I'D RATHER
SEE A SERMON

Showing Your Friends
the Way to Heaven

I'D RATHER SEE A SERMON

Showing Your Friends the Way to Heaven

Dave Stone

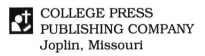
COLLEGE PRESS
PUBLISHING COMPANY
Joplin, Missouri

The poem "I'd Rather See a Sermon," by Edgar A. Guest (1881-
1959) is quoted from Dr. Paul Lee Tan's *Encyclopedia of 7700
Illustrations* (Assurance Publishers, Rockville, MD; now Bible
Communications, Dallas, TX), p. 1136, and is used by permis-
sion of the editor.

Library of Congress Cataloging-in-Publication Data

Stone, Dave, 1961–
    I'd rather see a sermon: showing your friends the way to
heaven / Dave Stone.
      p. cm.
    Includes bibliographical references.
    ISBN 0-89900-762-7 (pbk.)
    1. Witness bearing (Christianity) 2. Evangelistic work.
I. Title.
BV4520.S678 1996
248'.5—dc20   96-22879
                                     CIP

Dedicated

. . . to the memory of Bette Bowman,
the best mother-in-law a guy could ever want
A woman in whom you could see a sermon,
    who quietly preached God's truth through her life,
    who built bridges to lost and hurting people,
    and whose love for Christ, and people,
        lives on in my wife.

Table of Contents

I'd Rather See a Sermon

I'd rather see a sermon than hear one any day.
I'd rather one should walk with me than merely show the
way.
The eye's a better pupil and more willing than the ear;
Fine counsel is confusing, but example's always clear;
And the best of all the preachers are the men who live
their creeds;
For to see the good in action is what everybody needs.
I can soon learn how to do it if you'll let me see it done,
I can watch your hands in action, but your tongue too fast
may run.
And the lectures you deliver may be very wise and true;
But I'd rather get my lesson by observing what you do.
For I may misunderstand you and the high advice you
give,
But there's no misunderstanding how you act and how
you live.

—Edgar A. Guest.

Introduction

Society is changing so quickly it will make your head spin. But churches tend to run a decade or two behind the times. We're excited when our church buys a bus, when the world has already made the switch to vans. We're proud of our electric typewriter while modern technology has moved the masses On-line. We brag about buying a fax machine for the church office, while the members wonder when we're going to get E-mail. When it comes to winning the world to Christ, it is hard to reach a compact disc culture with 8-track methodology.

As times have changed, so have people. In *Time* magazine, Robert Wright said, "These days, thanks to electric garage-door openers, you can drive straight into your house, never risking contact with a neighbor" ("The Evolution of Despair," *Time* Aug. 28, 1995, p. 54). He's right. We used to build a front porch with a swing, now we build a back deck with a privacy fence.

Perceptive people realize that for the church to impact the community it will take effort and planning. There must be a desire to be on the cutting edge, and a willingness to try new ideas. Nowadays door to door evangelism, calling nights, and two-week revivals can reach a few, but most people will not be receptive to that approach.

The most exciting news is that to reach the lost, one

doesn't have to compromise any scriptural principle! Jesus said for us to be as wise as serpents and as harmless as doves (Matthew 10:16). Jesus' plan for lifestyle evangelism coupled with creative and current methods still works today. He wants us to live out our sermons!

Effective Methods

When you were growing up, whose face did you see on your box of Wheaties®? Be careful, your answer will reveal your age. Michael Jordan, Mary Lou Retton, Bruce Jenner, Cathy Rigby, Mark Spitz, Johnny Bench, Bart Starr (I'll stop there). Today if you were to sit down in front of a box of Wheaties whose face would you see? Shaquille O'Neal. Do you know why? Because Bart Starr's face doesn't sell cereal in the '90s.

The product is the same — Wheaties. The slogan is the same — "Breakfast of Champions." But the *marketing* method changed because society has changed. One of the changes has been that Christian leaders don't have the credibility that they once did, and Christians are painted with a broad brush as closed-minded fundamentalists.

But regardless of the accusations of the world or the misconceptions of people, our "product" is still the same — Jesus Christ. And people are not nearly as moved to accept Christ by a paid professional speaking from a pulpit, as they are by a genuine believer from the pew who fleshes out Christianity.

We are to be missionaries in the marketplace. Paul commissions all Christians to be ambassadors to the world in 2 Corinthians. Bill Hybels says, "There are too many ambassadors hanging out in the embassy." He's right.

Jesus *called* us in to *send* us out. Jesus didn't tell the world to go to church; He told the church to go to the world.

Some say, "Well, that's not my style. It isn't right to interfere in the lives of others. They're adults, they can make their own decisions. After all, it's not Christian to be nosy." (My wife thinks I'm nosy. She hasn't really come right out and said it, but the other day when she was out of the house, I read it in her diary!)

Even at the risk of being called nosy, we need to take a genuine interest in those around us. There is a big difference between putting your nose in other people's business and putting your heart in other people's problems.

Different Approaches

This book has been designed to show you a variety of approaches to sharing your faith with others. Different people will respond to different methods. *I'd Rather See a Sermon* is intended to be:

- ✧ a look at biblical examples of how to reach the lost
- ✧ an instruction for those who truly want to adapt their methods but not their message
- ✧ a sober challenge to those who "think" they are Christians
- ✧ an encouragement for the one who may be considering Christianity
- ✧ an inspiration to all who read it
- ✧ a reward for all who apply it

The bottom line is that sharing our faith must be a priority in our Christian life. Jesus Christ is the only hope for this world. Our message is salvation, our mission is evangelism, our time is now.

Lost and Found

A number of years ago, a couple was shopping in a department store in a large mall. They were looking at clothing when they realized that their five-year-old son

13

was nowhere to be found. So they began frantically searching for him. Some of the clerks even joined in the hunt. After a few minutes they heard a voice over the public address system say, "Would Mr. and Mrs. Bernard Johnson please report to the manager's office on the second floor." The couple immediately went bounding up the escalator and located the manager's office. As they burst through the door, there sat their son behind the manager's desk drinking a cola and having the time of his life. But when he saw the panicked look of fear on their faces the boy immediately burst into tears. Do you know why? The reality was, he had no idea he was *lost* until he was *found.*

A lot of people are in a spiritual condition which is very similar to that. We are surrounded by them — individuals who have never calculated the spiritual risk they are taking. They reason, "I'm a good person." But make no mistake: there are good people who are lost people. That's why we must feel a compulsion to get the message out. We must teach them that people don't go to heaven because of their goodness; they go to heaven because He is gracious. They must be willing to swallow their pride, and admit that they need a Savior.

The Christian's task is to reach the lost; those who have never made Christ the Lord of their life. We must do that as creatively and clearly as posssible. As Paul put it, "To the weak I became weak, to win the weak. I have become all things to all men so that by all possible means I might save some" (1 Corinthians 9:21-22). Win the lost, whatever the cost.

Maybe you heard about the overzealous preacher who would hang out on city buses and try to frighten people into making a decision for the Lord. One day a drunk stumbled onto the bus. The preacher sprang into action. He began to shake his oversized Bible in the face of the drunk. While pointing a finger of condemnation, he barked, "Did you know you're headed for hell?"

14

The drunk's face sank as he said, "Oh no, I'm on the wrong bus again!" You see, the world doesn't need to be told it's going to hell. The world needs to be shown how to get to heaven. That's where you come in.

I hope that this book teaches you how to stress commitment rather than coercion; devotion rather than duty; and love rather than obligation. Your friends whom you seek to reach need to see that Christianity is a lifestyle of freedom and enjoyment. It truly is the abundant life.

My prayer is that this book will help you do just that. May the seeds you plant — and the sermons you live — on behalf of Christ fall on fertile soil.

The Mandate:

Sermons to
Be Seen

When the Heat Is On

A fire blazed out of control in a small town nestled in a tiny valley. Several fire trucks had already arrived from neighboring towns, each driving to the top of the hill and stopping. None were willing to drive down into the raging inferno.

As the firemen and townspeople stood by, helplessly watching the buildings go up in flames, a dilapidated fire truck came lumbering down the road. The firemen all wore overalls and the truck itself looked fifty years old.

The old truck chugged up the hill and without even pausing at the top, it plunged over the hill right down into the middle of the fire. The men jumped off and began to fight the fire like wild men. The others stared in disbelief at their courage. Within minutes they had the flames under control. The town was saved; the firefighters were heroes.

A week later the town held a celebration in their honor. The mayor presented the fire chief with a check for $1,000 to his fire department. The mayor asked the chief, "What do you intend to do with the money?"

Without hesitation, the old fellah replied, "Well, the first thing we're gonna do is get those brakes fixed on our truck."

What do you do when the heat is on? Do you boldly

meet the situation head-on, or do you do your best to avoid the confrontation by slamming on the brakes? We all have opportunities to point people in the right direction. Your choice may determine whether people just hear sermons or if, through you, they are able to see a sermon.

In this chapter we're going to take a look at three Hebrew men who had their faith tested by a furious king and a fiery furnace. Like the fire department they went right on in without hesitation. But in this situation, it was no accident; it was on purpose. They were unsure of their future, but they were quite sure about their God. Their faith impacted an entire nation.

The Story

The book of Daniel begins with Nebuchadnezzar, king of Babylon, conquering Jerusalem and taking hostage a number of its finest young men to be used as servants to the king. For three years these young Hebrew slaves were trained for the king's service.

During that time, four men rose to the top: Daniel, Shadrach, Meshach, and Abednego. "In every matter of wisdom and understanding about which the king questioned them, he found them ten times better than all the magicians and enchanters in his whole kingdom" (Daniel 1:20).

Later, Daniel was promoted by King Nebuchadnezzar for correctly interpreting a dream. At Daniel's request, the king appointed Shadrach, Meshach, and Abednego as administrators over the province of Babylon. It was a rapid rocket to stardom for these Hebrew slaves.

But a major problem arose: Nebuchadnezzar had a ninety-foot tall golden image built. The people were to fall down and worship the image of gold. The penalty for refusing to worship the king's god was death in a blazing furnace. Shadrach, Meshach, and Abednego had a solid belief in the One True God Jehovah. To continue to follow Him could be hazardous to their health.

They were faced with two choices: bend and bow or stand and suffer. These three were well acquainted with God's command to worship Him only. But the peer pressure had to be incredible. "All the peoples, nations and men of every language fell down and worshiped the image of gold that King Nebuchadnezzar had set up" (Daniel 3:7).

Some astrologers came to the king and denounced these three stubborn Jews. They were shrewd. They thought, "If we get them thrown out, then we can be promoted." The astrologers were quick to point out how the three had disobeyed. This was not welcome news to the self image of the king. His anger burned at these insubordinates who chose their God over his.

Nebuchadnezzar said, "Is it true, Shadrach, Meshach and Abednego, that you do not serve my gods or worship the image of gold I have set up? . . . if you do not worship it, you will be thrown immediately into a blazing furnace. Then what god will be able to rescue you from my hand?" (Daniel 3:14,15).

If you were allowed to disobey God once in your entire life, this would be the time. But Shadrach, Meshach, and Abednego refused to take a "mulligan." Notice there are no protests. No pleas for mercy. And it is quite obvious that King Nebuchadnezzar was not in the mood for a rational discussion on civil liberties and religious freedom. The credibility of his office (not to mention his pride) had been damaged, so he responded in anger.

Nebuchadnezzar was so hot, that he had the furnace heated up seven times hotter than normal. In fact, when the strong soldiers threw these men into the fire, it was so hot that the soldiers died from the heat in the furnace entrance!

At this time I imagine the astrologers are probably saying, "Oh, King, you sure took care of them. Uh, when can we move into our new offices?" Just then the king experienced the shock of a lifetime. Instead of seeing *three* people in the fire, Nebuchadnezzar saw *four* unbound and unharmed. He said, "The fourth looks like a son of the gods" (Daniel 3:25).

I wonder what it was that made the fourth man look like deity. There must have been something special that even a pagan king could recognize. Evidently Shadrach, Meshach and Abednego were moving freely about even though they had been bound. The cords burned up but the men didn't.

(In my warped mind I envision them dancing around, celebrating this miracle by singing, "We Didn't Start the Fire.")

The king was so amazed at this miracle that he stood near the opening to the furnace and called, "Servants of the most high God, come out! Come here!"

Now it's good that I wasn't in that fire. I probably would have answered by saying, "Oh, King, I cannot hear you. Move a little closer!" But for these three, revenge was not part of their agenda.

The Bible says that after they came out they were quickly surrounded by the people who had come to watch the execution. They saw that the fire had not harmed the men in any way, not even a singed hair. (Remember, if God can save three men inside a blazing fire, He can remove the smoky smell.) When God does a miracle, He does it right.

There are so many principles from this story that you can apply in taking a stand for the Lord. Jesus gave a mandate to those who would choose to follow Him. He said, "Therefore go and make disciples of all nations, baptizing them in the name of the Father and of the Son and of the Holy Spirit, and teaching them to obey everything I have commanded you" (Matthew 28:19-20).

Stand Up and Be Recognized

Nowadays, if you're sold out for Christ you probably won't have to worry about the President throwing you into a blazing fire. But the committed Christian can expect to take some heat from a boss who expects you to be unethical, or a fiancee who tries to pressure you into being sexually active, with the line, "After all, we'll be married soon."

Do you choose to bend and bow or to stand up and be recognized? In order to be able to handle the heat of the furnace tomorrow you must be willing to stand for God today.

Steve Ropecki is a Christian businessman out in southern California. Les Christie tells of an incident several years ago when Steve was attending an insurance convention. The man who was speaking kept taking the Lord's name in vain over and over again.

Finally Ropecki had had more than he could take. So in the middle of the man's speech, he stood up on his chair, pointed at the speaker, and said, "You leave Christ out of it."

Ropecki sat back down and the man resumed speaking. He didn't take the Lord's name in vain again. But the amazing thing was, when he finished speaking, more people came up to shake Steve Ropecki's hand than they did the man who delivered the speech. You see, even the world recognizes those who are willing to take a stand. Peter Marshall said, "If a man's not willing to stand for something, then he's likely to fall for anything."

Shadrach, Meshach, and Abednego were in the minority. In fact, they were alone except for the One who promises He will never leave us. It's in those settings when God is expecting His followers to stand up and speak up. "Always be prepared to give an answer to everyone who asks you to give the reason for the hope that you have" (1 Peter 3:15).

Stand Out and Be Remembered

Christians are to be distinctive. Peter said that Christians are a "peculiar people, a holy nation" (1 Peter 2:9, KJV). His point is valid. What is the purpose of the church if we live like the rest of the world?

Missionary Dennis Free tells of a plague that swept through Indonesia. Countless people died. A number of Christians lost their children. He said, "It was tempting to be frustrated and ask God why He would shoot himself in the foot. But the reality was that people came to Christ, when they saw how the Christians maintained peace while burying their children."

They were distinctive. Notice with Shadrach, Meshach and Abednego there were no "Next time we'll bow, we promise" speeches. Instead, there was just peace and acceptance that God is in control.

Those who stand out are remembered for having the courage to resist the crowd. Robert Frost said, "Two roads diverged in a wood, and I — I took the one less travelled by, and that has made all the difference."*

Jesus said, "Enter through the narrow gate. For wide is the gate and broad is the road that leads to destruction, and many enter through it. But small is the gate and narrow the road that leads to life, and only a few find it. (Matthew 7:13,14)

It's like the 90-year-old man who was asked if it becomes easier to live the Christian life the older you get. He thought for a minute and then replied, "Well, there's a lot less peer pressure!" Most of us would rather fit in, than stand out. Christ is expecting us to stand out so that people can see the difference.

---

*Robert Frost, in *The Poetry of Robert Frost*, ed. Edward Connery Lathem (Toronto: Holt, Rinehart, and Winston, 1967), p. 105.

Stand Firm and Be Respected or Rejected

Throughout the course of the Christian life you are faced with opportunities, through your lifestyle, to either confess Christ or reject Him.

Although I was a leader at my high school, at times my Christian commitment needed a little encouragement. I found myself feeling comfortable praying in a restaurant when I was surrounded by my church youth group, but wimping out in the school cafeteria when surrounded by my non-Christian friends. That inconsistency began to bother me. I found that the best inspiration for living for Christ at school was the example of other believers who were more than willing to stand firm.

There was a girl who went to the same school as I did. Everyone knew where she stood with the Lord. Sometimes as I would be making my way through the cafeteria line, my stomach would start to churn. I knew that in a matter of minutes I would be faced with a decision — to pray or not to pray.

Regularly, I would scan the cafeteria looking for Gail Foster. Day after day she would bow her head and discreetly and silently thank God for her food. It might sound funny but her willingness to stand firm was a powerful witness to me. Although she didn't know it until years later, her example inspired me to stand firm. And I would venture to say that a lot of people knew of our convictions through that simple act of thanking God for our food. (It opened a number of doors with friends to talk about church and the Lord.)

Now I'm not suggesting that before you eat your lunch in the employee break room that you stand on a chair, ask everyone to bow their heads, and say, "Where He leads me I will follow; what He feeds me I will swallow." That might let others know where you stand, but it would probably

25

turn more people off! Remember, you don't *drive* people to Jesus, you *lead* them.

I doubt that God's first question on the Day of Judgment will be, "How 'bout those restaurant prayers?" Please understand, for me, it became a question of consistency versus hypocrisy. Jesus said, "Whoever acknowledges me before men, I will also acknowledge before my Father in heaven" (Matthew 10:32).

King Nebuchadnezzar said, "Therefore I decree that the people of any nation or language who say anything against the God of Shadrach, Meshach and Abednego be cut into pieces and their houses be turned into piles of rubble, for no other god can save in this way" (Daniel 3:29).

A few minutes earlier the three were "dead meat" because of their beliefs. Now the king says, "If you say anything against their God, then I'll have your body cut into pieces. And if that's not bad enough, on top of that, we'll tear down your house!" (Personally, after you cut me into pieces — I couldn't care less what you do to my house!)

Nebuchadnezzar was a man of extremes. Because of the faith of these three young men, the king made a 180-degree turn and changed the decree for an entire nation.

Shadrach, Meshach, and Abednego could have said to themselves, "Hey, is it really going to matter if we bow just this one time? Who's going to know? God really won't mind if we physically bow to this statue. He knows our hearts. It's not that big a deal!"

Have you ever felt that way? When the filthy stories start, or when the bottle's passed, or when you're filling out your tax returns . . . do you find yourself asking those kinds of questions?

Is it really going to make a difference in my relationship with God if I give in this one time? . . . if I run this person down behind his back

. . . if I keep watching the movie

. . . if I continue indulging in that secret sin every now and then?

The problem with that logic is that before you know it, those few-and-far-between incidents become more frequent occurences. Soon they are part of your everyday life. Yes, God knows your heart, but the Bible tells us that your actions and words are a reflection of what is truly inside your heart.

Will it really make a difference just this once? Yes. Will a weekend fling or an uncontrolled outburst really damage my witness? Yes. Because whether we realize it or not, the heart bows, long before the knee bends.

Lessons from the Furnace

Expect Heat

You don't have to call the psychic hotline in order to know you're going to face trials. Jesus said, "In this world you will have trouble. But take heart! I have overcome the world" (John 16:33).

There are issues that arise in your work environment and in your daily conversations which bring you the opportunity to let others know where you stand. I received a call recently from a young lady who belongs to the church where I serve. She was trying to start a prayer group at her job. It would not be on company time, and it would be purely voluntary. But she mentioned that a few people had said that they were against it.

I told her that she has to expect that. Satan isn't going to roll over and play dead because she chooses to seek creative ways to advance the gospel. But I also told her, "I wouldn't be surprised if, in a few months, one of those individuals who is against your prayer group might face a crisis, and ask to have their name added to your prayer list!"

Expect heat, but with it remember that God is still in control. Warren Wiersbe says, "When God permits His children to go through the furnace, He keeps his eye on the clock and His hand on the thermostat."

Contemporary Christian artist Rich Mullins has a song that says, "You'll meet the Lord in the furnace a long time before you meet Him in the sky."* Expect heat.

Exercise Faith

The apostle Paul was the New Testament equivalent of Shadrach, Meshach and Abednego when it came to standing up for his faith. Everywhere he went he started a riot or a revival — and sometimes both.

The writer of Hebrews said, "Now faith is being sure of what we hope for and certain of what we do not see" (Hebrews 11:1). Jesus taught that faith, even small amounts of it, could be quite potent. In other words, God is not impressed with the excuse, "Well, there's only a handful of Christians here. What could we possibly accomplish?" This story in Daniel 3 answers that question. Here were three men.

Thanks to their faith, a royal decree for an entire nation was reversed to stop pagan worship and promote the worship of the One True God.

Let me ask you something! Do people know where you stand spiritually, or is attending church and reading Christian literature only an effort to satisfy the expectations of some "religion"? Sure it is frightening to take a stand for Christ in today's culture. But the only cure for fear is faith.

---

*Rich Mullins, "Where You Are," The World As Best As I Remember It, Volume I, Reunion Records, 1991.

Exalt Christ

In his book, *When God Doesn't Make Sense,** James Dobson says, "It is comforting to note that only Shadrach, Meshach, and Abednego came out of the fire. That other Man, whom we believe to have been the Christ, remained there to comfort and protect you and me when we go through our fiery trials."

As I recounted this Bible story in this chapter, I intentionally skipped over the highlight of the story. You might be thinking, "No, you didn't. Three guys were thrown in a fire, and thanks to God's power and their faith, they lived to tell about it." But that's not it.

The highlight is not at the end of the story, it's in the middle of the story just before these three Hebrew men are thrown in the fire. If you'll allow me to paraphrase:

Nebuchadnezzar was feeling his oats, and he mocked the faith of Shadrach, Meshach and Abednego. He said, "Hey, if you don't worship the image I made, then you'll be tossed into the fiery furnace, and then what god will be able to rescue you?"

Shadrach, Meshach and Abednego replied, "Our God is able to save us — if He chooses. But even if he chooses not to save us, we're still going to serve Him" (Daniel 3:15-18). You see, *that's* the highlight. Regardless of the outcome, regardless of your well-being, you must trust Him more than you trust yourself. Not only was Babylon affected by their example, but so was the king.

The Allied forces were searching an abandoned house in Germany following World War II. Inside they saw where a victim of the holocaust had etched these words on a crumbling wall.

I believe in the sun, even when it does not shine.
I believe in love, even when it is not shown.

---

*James Dobson, *When God Doesn't Make Sense* (Wheaton: Tyndale House, 1993), p. 114.

I believe in God, even when He is silent.

Could you say with Shadrach, Meshach and Abednego, "Even if He chooses not to save me, I'm still going to serve Him"? Jesus said, "The man who loves his life will lose it, while the man who hates his life in this world will keep it for eternal life" (John 12:25).

The Bottom Line

Albert Schweitzer was on to something when he said, "Example is not the best way of teaching; it is the only way of teaching."

One of the things I have seen repeatedly in over 15 years of ministry is that people respond to the sermons they see. Perhaps that is why the apostle Paul said, "Follow my example, as I follow the example of Christ" (1 Corinthians 11:1). Time and time again I am reminded that, when faced with an ultimatum, the Christian must be willing to take a stand, regardless of the consequences.

When General Sherman made his infamous march to the sea, he wrought destruction everywhere he went. He and his troops came to a farmhouse where they found an older woman standing defiantly on the porch holding a broomstick in front of her.

General Sherman said, "Ma'am, you need to leave. We're about to burn your place down."

The woman said, "I'm not leaving."

Sherman pointed at the smoke behind him in the distance, and said, "Ma'am, you need to get some of your belongings. We're gonna burn this place down."

She gripped her broom tighter and repeated, "I'm not leaving."

Sherman said, "Do you really think that you can defeat the entire Union forces with a broomstick?"

"No, sir, she replied, I just want the world to know whose side I'm on."

When You Don't Want to Go

Perhaps you heard about the mother who called up to her son to get out of bed. "It's time to get ready for church!" He yelled back, "Mom, I'm not going." She said, "Why?" He replied, "The people are mean to me and the service is boring. Why should I go?"

"I'll give you two reasons," she shouted. "One, you're 40 years old; and two, you're the preacher!"

I don't want to go. How many times have you heard that response? How many times have you made that statement? Your friends choose a restaurant you can't stand, and you don't want to go. Your boyfriend plans to take you to see *Attack of the Killer Tomatoes*, and you had your heart set on seeing *Little Women*, so you don't want to go. In the middle of the night your spouse says it's your turn to put the pacifier in your five-month-old baby's mouth, and you don't want to go (purely hypothetical).

For an adult, it may be a tax audit, or a root canal; if you're a teenager, a family reunion or a funeral home. We all find ourselves in situations where we don't want to go. At times, those situations are ones where you sense that the Lord desires for you to do something, but you really don't want to do it.

Jonah knew this feeling. He would have had a hard time singing and meaning, "I'll go where you want me to go, dear Lord."

Jonah's Story

The story of Jonah is more than a fish story, it's a faith story. We need to get past the novelty of the story and realize that it is saturated with positive teaching through a negative example. Jonah was a wayward missionary who was forced by God to face the prejudice and fear which kept him from telling others of salvation.

His story is in many ways the mirror image of our own aborted evangelistic efforts — opportunities where we have fearfully slammed a door which God has opened, placing us in the face of one who needs to hear the gospel.

The entire book is quite short. You can read all four chapters in the time it would take you to read "Green Eggs and Ham." Most of us are familiar with the story (Jonah, that is), at least the part about three days inside the fish. But the rest of the story may be a little fuzzy.

God Says Go!

The book begins with the Lord commanding Jonah to go to Nineveh and preach repentance to the wicked inhabitants of that city. But Jonah chose to run from the Lord. He went in the opposite direction to Tarshish. That choice clearly communicated to God, "I don't want to go." His sense of direction seemed to express his level of commitment. So Jonah found a ship and attempted to sail away from God's will.

In all fairness to Jonah, this was not a very pleasant assignment. Two logical reasons could explain his hesitation to obey. The first was prejudice. Nineveh was located at the heart of the Assyrian nation, the archenemy of Israel. The book of First Chronicles tells how Assyrian hordes made raids down into the land of the Israelites and committed heinous war crimes. These actions not only put terror in the hearts of the Jews but created extreme hatred toward that nation. Jonah felt that God was asking

32

too much when He told him to go and warn its capital city, Nineveh, of impending disaster. His attitude suggests, "If the city is destroyed, I wouldn't regret it." After all, they were just getting what they deserved.

The second reason Jonah didn't want to go was fear. It was a simple exercise in self-preservation. If he obeyed God's command, it could mean physical harm for him, and the thought of that didn't pump him up!

Jonah Says No!

So Jonah ran from God, by way of a boat. But God caught his attention by sending a great wind and a violent storm. Jonah admitted that he was running from the almighty God and that he was to blame for the storm. At Jonah's request the crew threw him overboard. This was their last-ditch effort at self-preservation. "But the LORD provided a great fish to swallow Jonah, and Jonah was inside the fish three days and three nights" (Jonah 1:17).

People argue whether or not the great fish was a whale, a shark, or something else. It is true that there have been several documented instances of a human being swallowed by a whale and surviving. But all of these well-intentioned explanations miss the point of the story. The point is that God is the worker of this miracle. He provided the great wind and He appointed the great fish.

From inside the fish Jonah prayed to the Lord (understatement of the year for 862 B.C.). He spoke of his distress. He described what it is like to be hurled into the deep and engulfed in the waters.

Jonah 2:5 says that seaweed was wrapped around his head. (This is the first documented case of a "bad hair day"!) Being inside this fish gave Jonah plenty of time to make amends with God and to make some promises to him as well.

You can probably remember a time when your back

was to the wall and you made some promise to God. Mine was in eighth grade when it came time for three weeks of wrestling in gym class. Because I really hated the sport of wrestling, I made a promise to God that if I survived that time in wrestling, then upon my graduation I would go into the ministry!

The greatest fear of my life was being suffocated by another adolescent's armpit. We had to select a wrestling partner for the entire time. I picked the biggest wimp in the class — Tim Weisenhymer. (This is not his real name, just in case he has gained weight and joined the World Wrestling Federation!) I did survive and I kept my promise and entered the ministry. (It's not a real spiritual story, but none the less it's true.) Jonah made good on his promise too.

But I can think of countless promises I haven't kept. Can you? We've all heard them: "Lord, if the house sells, then I'll give 20% of the profits to You."

"God, if I get the job, I'll never miss coming to church."

"Lord, if it's benign, I'll thank You every day of my life."

People make vows in times of distress that they forget in times of security.

In *The Adventures of Tom Sawyer* you may recall that some of Tom's friends were converted in a revival meeting. They made big changes, but Tom only thought about it. Then that night there was a big storm. Tom Sawyer was convinced the storm was God punishing him for his failure to repent.

Mark Twain wrote, "By and by the tempest spent itself and died without accomplishing its object. The boy's first impulse was to be grateful, and reform. His second was to wait — for there might not be any more storms."*

We make promises in storms that we later forget. But

---

*Mark Twain, *The Adventures of Tom Sawyer* (Pleasanton, NY: Readers Digest Association, 1985), p. 144.

Jonah vowed to God that if he got out alive he would be faithful. "What I have vowed I will make good" (Jonah 2:9).

Someone said, "There are no atheists in foxholes." Humorist Lewis Grizzard expanded that statement for golf lovers to say, "There are no atheists in sand traps." I would add, "There are no atheists inside of the belly of a fish!" The longer he was inside, the more sincere his promises became.

Jonah made a promise, and he wanted God to know that he meant business. (Had they known, the Bible college recruiters would have been camped on the shore complete with enrollment applications and bumper stickers!) The Bible tells us that God commanded the fish to vomit Jonah onto the dry land.

Even a big fish can't stomach a wayward prophet, and so it belched him onto the beach. Bob Russell says, "If this were a movie, Jonah would have landed in some sand next to a sign that said, Nineveh — Three Miles."

Jonah Says Woe!

"Jonah obeyed the word of the LORD and went to Nineveh. Now Nineveh was a very important city — a visit required three days. On the first day, Jonah started into the city. He proclaimed: 'Forty more days and Nineveh will be overturned.' The Ninevites believed God. They declared a fast, and all of them, from the greatest to the least, put on sackcloth" (Jonah 3:3-5).

Some serious preaching was going on. A major revival took place. Commentators project the population to have been about 600,000 people. It would be like Billy Graham coming to Louisville, Kentucky, and *everyone* repenting and committing their lives to Christ. In fact, the citizens of Nineveh took it so seriously that, not only did they pray and fast, they even made their animals fast! (They weren't taking any chances!) The Bible says that they were broken because of their sins.

Jonah must have preached powerfully. One would think that such an overwhelming response to an invitation would be cause for a spiritual celebration. But not so. Jonah was so selfish and ethnocentric that he got mad.

"He prayed to the LORD, 'O LORD, is this not what I said when I was still at home? That is why I was so quick to flee to Tarshish. I knew that you are a gracious and compassionate God, slow to anger and abounding in love, a God who relents from sending calamity. Now, O LORD, take away my life, for it is better for me to die than to live'" (Jonah 4:2-3).

Can you believe that! Jonah began to have a pity party for himself. He actually thought, I've let my nation down. God, You're just too kind. All of my enemies spared. To make matters worse, You involved me in the salvation process. I'd be better off dead!

Jonah had become so preoccupied with himself and his people that he couldn't bring himself to look beyond the boundaries. Are we ever like that? Unwilling to cross a boundary or tear down a barrier in order to share the gospel.

Look around at your church. Do people of different ethnic backgrounds feel comfortable in your fellowship? Could a wealthy person and a poor person sit together in the same pew with both of them feeling convicted and encouraged by the preaching?

God Has the Last Word

Through the story of Jonah we see that even back in the Old Testament, God was laying the foundation for a New Testament principle — the ground is level at the foot of the cross. God told Jonah, "But Nineveh has more than a hundred and twenty thousand people who cannot tell their right hand from their left, and many cattle as well. Should I not be concerned about that great city?" (Jonah 4:11).

Jonah didn't want to go to Nineveh; when he did go, he didn't want them to repent. Then, when they did repent he wasn't happy. Not a real flattering story. Most commentators think, however, that Jonah must have made some significant changes in his life, or else the book would never have been included in God's Word. We can learn a positive lesson from a negative example. That is Jonah's story, and yet you can see some amazing similarities with our story.

Our Story

When it comes to sharing his faith, Jonah only had two excuses — but it's not that way with us! Today in our advanced culture we can come up with a whole pack of reasons. Some people are too proud to tell others of their beliefs for fear of being labeled a fanatic. Norman Vincent Peale once said, "Everyone who ever followed Christ became a fisher of men. If you are not fishing, then you are not following."

Others rationalize their "I don't want to go" attitude by misinterpreting circumstances to be divine revelations. Notice that everything seemed to go smoothly for Jonah at first. When he arrived at Joppa he was fortunate enough to find a ship ready to sail in the opposite direction (to Tarshish). Tickets were available, and he easily booked passage.

Favorable circumstances might lead a superficial person to believe that God was blessing. Sometimes I hear people say, "I know you're thinking it's an affair and I shouldn't be having it, but if you only knew how miserable I have been and how well things have clicked for us, then you would know that this has to be from God. He has led

37

us to each other." Someone else says, "I got pregnant, but it was so simple to obtain an abortion. My grandmother offered to pay for it. Nobody really seemed to object."

Don't always interpret favorable circumstances as the path of God. It may just be the calm before the storm which is ready to break upon a rebellious servant of God.

One self-righteous church member proudly came up to his minister after a sermon and said, "You know, Preacher, Satan never seems to bother me or tempt me. In fact, it's as if he doesn't even exist." To which the wise minister replied, "Two people walking down the same path, in the same direction seldom bump into each other." Sometimes we get so far off course that what looks favorable is, in actuality, potential disaster.

Another popular excuse is to plead ignorance. With all of the great Bible study helps and the wealth of information at our fingertips, I'm certain that this excuse must get old to God. Instead of trying to study the Word and deepen their knowledge of the truth, for decades some Christians continue to use this excuse.

Others feebly cling to what is left of their self-image. They don't share their faith for fear of being ridiculed. They buy into Satan's lie, "Your friends will laugh at you." But the believer must remember: Jesus didn't promise His followers a rose garden. Matthew 16:24 reminds us that He promised a cross.

The truth of the matter is that Christians *will* be ridiculed if they are actively testifying on behalf of Christ. Jesus said, "Woe to you when all men speak well of you, for that is how their fathers treated the false prophets" (Luke 6:26). Expect ridicule. It comes with the territory. But it doesn't compare to being crucified on a cross.

The Number One Excuse

Probably the number one reason that Christians say, "I

don't want to," when it comes to evangelism is apathy. It's easy to shirk our responsibility and compromise our commitment. We choose to take the easy way out: risk-free living, "secret-service Christianity." Regardless of which excuse you or I tend to use to rationalize our indifference, none of them hold water. Running away from God's will is disobedience. Period!

Dr. Rollo May says, "Man is the strangest creature of all. He's the only one who runs faster when he loses his own way." (Wives might add, "And they are too proud to stop and ask for directions.") At times we've all headed to Tarshish when God commanded us to go to Nineveh. We don't want to go to people or places where we clearly felt God encouraging us to share the gospel.

Maybe yours was a relationship that you were challenged to restore, but you chose silence. Maybe it was the Lord's calling you into some type of vocational Christian service, but you chose to seek your own agenda. Maybe your Nineveh was the home of a relative who needed you to explain the gospel, but you chose the easy road — Complacency Avenue. Don't rock the boat and get the family in an uproar.

Getting Back on Course

Regardless of the opportunities you may have bypassed in the past, it is not too late to get back on course. A few years ago I spoke at a conference in St. Louis. They have a belt line highway that circles the city. In the extreme left lane a sign reads, "Express Lane." People in the lanes on the right were creeping along at about 40 miles per hour, so I whipped over into the "Express Lane." It was great! I was passing dozens of cars over in the slow lanes. Now I was a little fuzzy on my directions, but I was in the "Express Lane." I had no idea where I was going, but I was making great time!

After I'd been on it for a while I saw the exit that I was supposed to take. But there was one problem. One of the privileges you forfeit in the fast lane is that you can't exit whenever you want. A cement barrier separates you from the other lanes. About every eight miles they allow you an opportunity to get over to the right and exit. So I had to drive right past my exit and stay in the "Express Lane" for another four miles traveling in the wrong direction, get off on another exit, sit through a couple of traffic lights, hop back on the interstate, get in the "turtle lane," and creep back for four miles.

I was able to get back on the right path, but it cost me about fifteen precious minutes. Jonah came back, the prodigal son came back, and we can too — but it's going to cost you something. It might cost you time, opportunities, or maybe even your health.

Some commentators speculate that it cost Jonah his appearance. Three days inside the belly of a fish doesn't do much for your complexion. (That's usually not a turn-on to the female population. "You spent three days tumbling in the gastric juices of a mammal. Come get close to me, you hunk!")

For the prodigal son it cost him respect. It probably took years to regain the trust of his community. Harry Emerson Fosdick was right: "After all, one thing is far better than bringing the Prodigal Son back from the far country, and that is keeping him from going there in the first place."*

As you read this chapter, many of you can relate. You've tried life in the fast lane and now you're heading back to Nineveh in the direction of God's will. How far out of the way did you go? How long did it take you to turn around and head for home? Or have you even put your blinker on and started to slow down to make that change?

---

*Harry Emerson Fosdick, *Riverside Sermons* (New York: Harper and Brothers, 1958), p. 85.

Is there someone you can help to get moving in the right direction?

Luke 15:20 says, "But while he was still a long way off, his father saw him and was filled with compassion for him; he ran to his son, threw his arms around him and kissed him." Which is it for you? Are you the one in need of reaching out to redirect another? Or are you the one in need of being embraced and forgiven? Either way, instead of wandering aimlessly God loves you and wants you back home with Him.

The Lessons to Be Learned

Keep the Big Picture in Mind

Jonah was so self-centered, he lost the big picture. He forgot that his priority was to win lost people to God, not to live a life of comfort or impress others. At times you may lose perspective too. Perhaps you focus entirely on yourself and don't see the impact your life can have on others.

God has a different measuring rod for success than the world has. His doesn't involve achievement, one's financial portfolio, or outward appearance. He looks at the heart. He wants us to see our task on earth as trying to lead others to heaven through a personal relationship with Christ. The poet said,

> When I get to that wonderful city,
> and the saints all around me appear,
> I want to have somebody tell me,
> it was you that invited me here!

You see, in the big scheme of things the temporal pales in comparison to the eternal.

God Disciplines Believers for Intentional Sin

We've all heard that there are two different types of sin

41

— sins of commission (willful acts of disobedience) and sins of omission (failure to do what the Bible teaches us to do). God warns us through the life of Jonah. Jonah persistently defied God's command and God brought discipline and stress into his life to teach him obedience.

There is a difference between willful sin and spontaneous sin. Even our judicial system differentiates between crimes of passion and those that are premeditated.

A small boy was told by his father not to go swimming in a nearby pond. When he came home with his hair all wet, his father reminded him that he had been told not to go in the pond. The boy said, "But I fell in!" His dad asked, "Then why aren't your clothes wet?" The boy said, "Well, I had a hunch I might fall in, so I took them off!"

There is a big difference between falling into sin and repeatedly plotting to sin. But God is not foolish. He knows when we are deliberately and persistently defying His Word. "If we deliberately keep on sinning after we have received the knowledge of the truth, no sacrifice for sins is left, but only a fearful expectation of judgment and of raging fire that will consume the enemies of God" (Hebrews 10:26-27). It's a condition of the heart.

God's Timetable Is Perfect

He can orchestrate a storm. He can plan the exact moment that a large fish comes by with a big mouth and a big appetite. He can microwave the time it takes for a plant to grow and provide shade for a prophet in order to teach him an important lesson. He's never late, never early. Whether you are waiting for a spouse, applying for a job, or hoping for a baby, His timetable is always perfect.

In the same way, some people's hearts are hardened to the gospel. Just about the time you feel that a friend for whom you've been praying for years will never be open to spiritual things, all of a sudden God can turn a hardened heart to fertile soil. I believe that God enjoys engineering "opportunities" for Christians to share their faith at just the right time.

I am very fortunate to serve at a church where it is very easy to invite people to attend. The services are excellent, the people are friendly, and the preaching is good (at least that's what my mother says).

Several years ago my wife was shopping at a mall and she overheard a young woman and an older woman talking about churches. The young woman said, "No, I won't go back there. I'm looking for a new church."

So a few minutes later, Beth said, "Are you really wanting to find a new church?" The young lady said emphatically, "Yes!" Beth said, "Because I would love to invite you to the church where I belong. It's Southeast Christian Church." Beth gave the lady her phone number and that night Nancy called. Soon she was attending church regularly.

About a year later, after getting involved in a Bible study, she made a commitment to Christ. I even had the privilege of baptizing her. Thanks to my wife's boldness and being perceptive, the good news is that now Nancy has a personal relationship with the Lord. The bad news is my wife feels that God has called her to minister in the malls! Last week she came home with six shopping bags in her hands. I said, "Where have you been?" And she said, "Oh, out sharing my faith!" I have continued to have a recurring nightmare, that Beth is going to start a new support group at our church called "Shoppers for the Savior"!

The timing of God is never late, never early — it is always perfect!

God Is Counting on You!

The book of Jonah is a book of evangelism. Evangelism

43

is just a fancy name for telling others the good news of Jesus Christ. Christians have a responsibility to share their faith.

God is counting on you to be open to His leading. You may be the only person who can reach a certain individual or group of people. God has planted you in that environment to accomplish His purpose for eternity.

Can you think of some people who not only need to *hear* the message of God's love, but desperately need to *see* it in your life? What has been your response? Schubert said, "What I possess in my heart I will share with the world." The Bible makes no bones about the fact that God is counting upon believers to spread the gospel. Just before his ascension Jesus told His followers, "You will be my witnesses in Jerusalem, and in all Judea and Samaria, and to the ends of the earth" (Acts 1:8).

In her book, *Out of the Saltshaker,* Becky Pippert says, "Christians and non-Christians have something in common: we're both uptight about evangelism."* Her point is valid. Christians are afraid of offending, and unbelievers are afraid of being assaulted.

Pippert points out that you don't have to fall in the category of audacity or timidity; there can be a balance. She encourages believers to build relationships with those who don't believe and to share with them your feelings of Christ without being pushy.

The first four years of our marriage, Beth and I rented the downstairs of a house in northern Kentucky. Our landlady was a woman in her seventies who lived upstairs. Her name was Elsie. She was the nicest, most generous woman you ever would meet. At that time I was working for a Bible college, traveling and preaching a lot on weekends. But on the weekends we were in town, we attended

---

*Rebecca Manley Pippert, *Out of the Saltshaker* (Downers Grove: InterVarsity Press, 1979), p. 15.

the Lakeside church which was just five minutes away.

When we moved to Louisville to minister at Southeast, a couple in our Sunday school class was looking for a place to rent. So we matched them up with Elsie and she agreed to let them replace us. About a year or so later I was reading through some mail. I came across the Lakeside church newsletter and I read where Elsie had made a decision for the Lord and joined the church.

I was so surprised and excited that I called up the church. One of the associate ministers told me that Chris and Pam (the couple who had moved in after us) had invited her to church. Elsie started coming and decided to make a commitment to Christ and be baptized. After I hung up the phone, I started rationalizing my guilt. Well, Dave, you were out of town preaching on a lot of weekends, and Elsie drove home to the country on a lot of weekends.

But there was one thing I couldn't get out of my mind. I knew why she had never come to our church. To me, it was obvious. I had never invited her. It's pretty difficult to reap a crop if you never sow any seed.

The Bottom Line

Like me, perhaps you can think of times when you bypassed an opportunity to share Christ. Regardless of past times when you may have said, "I don't want to go," it's not too late to begin to redeem the time and plant seeds on behalf of the Lord.

And before you are too hard on poor old Jonah, let's realize that evidently, later in life, he must have realized the immaturity of his actions and had a change of heart. God allowed his story to be contained in the Bible so that it would motivate us not to follow his negative example.

The burden of an unsaved world rests upon our shoulders. You may be the only person who can reach that golfing partner, that obnoxious neighbor, that disabled person, that belligerent boss. God has planted you in a certain place. What on earth are you doing for Heaven's sake? What is the sermon that can be seen in you?

Has the Lord laid someone on your heart? Even when you don't want to go — God is still counting on you! One man said it like this: "I'm just a nobody, trying to tell everybody, about Somebody, who can save anybody."

Building Bridges

Recently I found out that my daughter Sadie enjoys building bridges. You may be thinking, she must be a tomboy? Well, not exactly. She isn't too mechanically inclined, nor is she very skilled at putting things together. The bridges she builds are not physical, they are spiritual. Although at the time I'm writing this she has just turned four, she is consumed with concern for a person's spiritual condition. A daily question she routinely asks is, "Does _____ love Jesus?" The blank could be filled in with the name of a neighbor, a relative, or a total stranger that she has struck up a conversation with at a ball game!

Sadie has an evangelistic heart. She prays by name for people who don't yet "love Jesus." Last week she was grilling one of Beth's girlfriends about the girl's father. She said, "Is your dad a Christian?"

The gal answered, "Well, he goes to church some."

But Sadie didn't retreat; she continued, "But is he a Christian?"

And Beth's friend said, "Well, to be real honest, we're not real sure if he has a relationship with Jesus."

And as serious as can be Sadie replied, "Well, you need to talk to him!"

And the girl said, "You are exactly right, I will find out."

My wife and I hope that she will always have that passion for people and that innocence which wants everyone to "love Jesus" and be a Christian. She is off to a good start in building bridges to the unsaved. But the older she gets the more she will see that many people "play church." They darken the doorway in an attempt to pay their spiritual dues and relieve their guilt. But when it comes to having a personal relationship with Jesus, they don't.

Maybe you heard about the parrot who was part of a comedy act at a nightclub. Eventually the club went bankrupt and sold the building to a church, but no one bothered to tell the parrot. The next week he flew into the room that had become the sanctuary. He looked at the choir and said, "Ahh! New orchestra."

Then he looked at the preacher and said, "Ahh, we got a new emcee, new emcee."

Then the parrot looked at the congregation and said, "Ahh, same crowd!!"

The truth can be painful. The church serves no purpose if it looks the same as the rest of the world. Most people pay more attention to how you live than to what you say. Talk is cheap, that's why the world is wanting and waiting to see Christ in your life. That just may be the only sermon they ever see and the only bridge that is ever built for them.

Satan's Favorite Lie

One time a friend asked me what I thought was the most effective lie that Satan has promoted. It is tough to narrow it down to the top one; however, I did venture a guess. Call it an opinion or a hypothesis but this is the one that seems to distort so many people's understanding of Christianity:

> If you are a good person who believes in God and lives a good life then your eternity in heaven is secure.

Here's Satan's same message with a little different wording: as long as your good deeds outnumber your bad deeds on the chalkboard of life, you've got it made. What does the Bible have to say about that? "You believe that there is one God. Good! Even the demons believe that — and shudder" (James 2:19).

What does the author and perfector of our faith have to say about that? "I am the way, the truth and the life, no one comes to the Father except through me" (John 14:6).

The problem is that heaven is a perfect environment where no evil can enter. The only One who can build a bridge to eternity for the imperfect is the perfect son of God.

Who Needs a Bridge?

Maybe you heard about the little boy in Sunday School who was giving his teacher fits. Finally the exasperated leader couldn't take it any longer. He grabbed the unruly kid, and began to shake him. He said, "Boy, I think the devil's got a hold of you!" Feeling the grasp of his teacher the boy exclaimed, "So do I!"

The devil does have a hold on each of us, in different places to different degrees. The fact of the matter is we are all separated from God by sin.

Back in 1994 when the Whitewater scandal was at its height, the *Wall Street Journal* had a full page of brief editorials from figures involved in the Watergate scandal. Each commented on resemblances and differences between the "two gates."

I was so impressed with Chuck Colson's comments that I saved them. Colson was the former White House aide to President Nixon. Colson was convicted and went to prison. His slant on analyzing the situation was completely different from everyone else.

Colson, who since Watergate has become a Christian,

used the opportunity to remind readers of man's greatest problem — sin. Colson wrote:

> The most astonishing thing about Whitewater is that we are astonished by it. Our reaction . . . reveals how deluded we are about the most pernicious myth of this century: that man is good, and that with technology and education we can achieve utopian societies.
>
> Our founders were not so naive. They understood the Judeo-Christian truth that man is a sinner. . . . Not to minimize wrongdoing, only to understand it, one should recognize that, like it or not, governors do make cozy deals and White House aides are by nature — I know — overzealous (March 11, 1994, *Wall Street Journal*).

The devil really does have a hold on each of us, whether you are a salesman or a security guard; a president or a preacher. Contrary to all the political rhetoric, society is getting worse instead of better. There is no need to substantiate that statement with documentation of statistics and quotes. Just visit your nearest public school and talk to a teacher who has been there for twenty years. Or pick up your newspaper and read of the problem of overcrowded jails, and early release programs for even violent offenders.

Christ is the only hope. He is the only way, and the only one who can bridge the distance between emptiness and fulfillment, from hell to heaven.

Our Moral Dilemma

I like the way Rick Warren, mega-church minister in Mission Viejo, California, explains our moral dilemma. His simple explanation centers around a popular book which came out a couple of decades ago. In the book entitled, *I'm Okay, You're Okay*, the author, Thomas Harris, speaks of four ways you can treat people. First you can treat them like, "I'm okay, you're okay." The second way is,

"I'm okay, but you're not okay." The third way is, "I'm not okay, but you're okay." The final approach that the book studied was, "I'm not okay and you're not okay."

The premise of the book was that everyone should act as if, "I'm okay, and you're okay." That is a concept known as transactional analysis. It sounds nice and looks good in print. There's just one problem. The premise, "I'm okay, you're okay" is a false one. Rick Warren concludes by saying, "The New Testament teaches this: I'm not okay. You're not okay. But because of Jesus that's okay."

You don't go to heaven because of your goodness, but because of Christ's graciousness. The Christian has the hope of heaven because of the promise that says, "Therefore, there is now no condemnation for those who are in Christ Jesus" (Romans 8:1).

Paul wrote those words because, better than anyone else he knew that accomplishments can't reserve a place in a heaven. Like many people today, Paul had enough morality to keep him out of trouble, but not enough righteousness to get him into heaven.

When I was growing up, my brother and I loved to go to an amusement park right outside of Cincinnati. King's Island, in our opinion, had it all. In its first few years of existence the "Racer" was the park's only roller coaster. As soon as we would arrive we would run to the Racer. Before you could get on it you had to stand next to a wooden figurine of Donald Duck to see if you were tall enough to ride. My brother Jeff was two years older than I was and he towered about six inches over his younger, vertically challenged brother.

The first few times we went I missed the height requirement by a number of inches. My brother just missed it by an inch. But the truth still remained, neither one of us could ride the Racer, because neither one of us measured up. According to the rule, it really didn't matter if you missed it by a foot or an inch, there was still a gap that we could not bridge.

The same is true with heaven. Heaven is a perfect place and it doesn't matter if you have committed a thousand sins or just a few, the truth remains — imperfection cannot reside in a perfect environment. Paul taught the church at Rome that no one could measure up to the Law. He wrote, "For all have sinned and fall short of the glory of God" (Romans 3:23).

James echoed Paul's thoughts when he wrote, "For whoever keeps the whole law and yet stumbles at just one point is guilty of breaking all of it" (James 2:10). So who needs a bridge? The answer is — every one of us.

Jesus Built a Bridge

But God realized our dilemma and so He sent Jesus to build a bridge to make up the remaining distance. The Bible says, "The blood of Jesus, his Son, purifies us from all sin" (1 John 1:7).

Recently our church held its annual Easter pageant. The music was powerful; the singing stirred your heart. We even had two real camels (you knew they were real by the smell). The guy who played Jesus was awesome.

The pageant went through the birth of Christ, His ministry, the healings, the death, burial, resurrection and ascension. Through the program you really could see and sense the incredible love that Christ has for you.

One night there was an Asian couple with a Hindu background who were visiting. They were moved by the program. But after the pageant, guess what they said to the people behind them? The couple said, "Excuse me, is this story true?"

The people reassuringly said, "Oh, yes, it is true."

You don't have to travel overseas on a mission trip in order to find people who are unacquainted with the account of the life of Jesus Christ. And they certainly don't have to have come from another culture! Don't be surprised when you discover that they live in your neighborhood and sit in your breakroom. Maybe you are the bridge builder who can introduce them to the peace and joy which comes from having a relationship with the Lord.

How Do You Build a Bridge?

When it comes to sharing your faith, your style could be compared to either a shark, a carp or a dolphin. All three are very different in their approach to life. In his book on evangelism entitled, *Conspiracy of Kindness*, Steve Sjogren says, "Sharks don't just live life, they attack it! . . . Sharks tend to traumatize everyone around them with their unfettered aggression. . . . Sharks tend to fit the picture of all the worst characteristics of a pushy salesman."*

I'm sure you've known some people who fit that description when it comes to evangelism. They have such a passion for winning the lost quickly that their aggression and forthrightness can turn off those who are in their path! Rather than building a bridge to Christ they alienate individuals through confrontation and intimidation.

But the pendulum swings all the way to the other side. Sjogren suggests that there are some Christians whose view of evangelism is more comparable to a carp. He writes, "Carp move through life in a lethargic manner. They see themselves as life's victims, too weak to ever function as a change-agent in life. . . . Carp don't make things happen, they watch things happen."†

I've known a number of Carp Christians who view winning the lost as the preacher's job but not theirs. They

---

*Steve Sjogren, *Conspiracy of Kindness* (Ann Arbor, MI: Servant, 1993), p. 35.

†Ibid., p. 38.

never run the risk of offending a friend or turning some-one off with the gospel, mainly because they never share it. Their attitude is, "You come to me and then maybe I can point you in the direction of someone who can help."

The final animal is the balance which we are striving for in our efforts to build a bridge to the lost. Sjogren says, "Dolphins combine the strengths of sharks and carps. These people are enthusiastic and positive about life, yet keep the issue of personal responsibility in proper bal-ance. The dolphin moves through life with a deep sense of purpose, whereas the shark tends to be overly responsible and the carp accomplishes little or nothing. The dolphin has a mission in life, but still has fun on the way to the goal."*

Sharing your faith shouldn't be a chore to you. Hopefully the more you do it the more natural it will become. You will become better at building bridges to the lost, the more you use the dolphin's approach.

Is There Still Time to Build Bridges?

This society is getting more wicked by the hour. Christian principles and an openness to the gospel by soci-ety as a whole are things of the past. The moral decay is all around. The next generation will have to reap the fall-out from Godless decisions which this generation has made. You can't rebuild a culture overnight. I agree with Thomas Sowell who said, "Once you open the floodgates, you cannot tell the water where to go."† And so the moral decay continues and more and more people drift further and further from the bridge.

Some time ago our family was enjoying an afternoon at

---

*Ibid., p. 39.

†Quoted by Austin Pryor in *Sound Mind Investing*, March 1994, edi-torial, p. 135.

a swimming pool. I was down in the deep end by the diving board. My daughter Savannah was four at the time. She came down the steps that lead into the shallow end. She was wearing those big orange floaties on her arms that keep her above the water.

As soon as she came off the last step she was kind of bobbing around and she looked across the pool at me and yelled, "Daddy, I'm scared. I want to come down where you are."

I kind of laughed at her naivete, and I said, "But Savannah, it's a lot deeper down here."

She called back, "I don't care, I want to be with you."

I said, "Okay, come on."

And so Savannah started dog paddling across the pool, three feet deep, six feet deep, nine feet deep, twelve feet deep. When she came up to grab hold of my neck her look of panic gave way to a look of relief. Do you realize why? Because next to her father she felt secure, and to her it made very little difference how deep or dangerous the water was.

Spiritual warfare is not something that is coming — it's here. Life in these United States is difficult. There are more risks and dangers. Satan and his society keep trying to pull us under and the water keeps getting deeper and deeper. That's why it's imperative we stay close to the Father and experience His power and peace. The times are tough, and there are lost people who desperately need bridges, but don't forget — you yourself must remain afloat, and with God's help keep your head above water.

The Bottom Line

Perhaps the first verse you ever memorized was John 3:16. Jesus said, "For God so loved the world that he gave his one and only Son, that whoever believes in him shall not perish but have eternal life." You might summarize that verse by saying, Jesus came to earth to build a bridge.

Your response must be to accept His offer and believe in Him. Your challenge is to build bridges to the lost through what you say and how you live. For when that happens, you will be carrying out the mandate which Christ commissioned His followers to perform. Then your lips and lifestyle can enable people to *see* sermons as opposed to just hearing them.

The Methods:

Seeds to Be Sown

Seeds, Soils and Sowing

Some people say, "It doesn't matter what you believe, we're all headin' for the same place!" Don't believe that. Jesus taught something completely different. He said, "I am the way and the truth and the life. No one comes to the Father except through me" (John 14:6). Evidently, Jesus wasn't real big on multicultural views! While He is the only way, there are different methods which can lead a person to the way, Jesus Christ.

Jesus himself modeled a number of methods for reaching the lost. His own ministry proved the value of flexibility in methods.

Methods are many, Principles are few,
Methods always change, Principles never do.

If you are a Christian, think about it — how were you reached for Christ? Probably it would be difficult to pinpoint one way. Usually it is a combination of several different touches.

The challenge is to take the gospel which never changes to a world that is constantly changing. Look with me at some of the different methods which Jesus used in His daily encounters with lost people.

Current Methods

Jesus' teaching was fresh. He used everyday illustrations and examples that people could relate to. Some time ago General Norman Schwartzkopf spoke at a business convention in Louisville. After he had been talking for about ten minutes he said, "All I've done so far is preach a sermon, but now I'm going to get practical." (Makes you wonder what type of preaching he has been exposed to.)

Jesus modeled practical, everyday preaching. True preaching is relevant. When the gospel is shared out of pure motives, it will be energized by the Holy Spirit, so that throughout the week as you go about your life, you are reminded of different analogies, comments, and Scriptures that coincide with what you are facing.

One of the biggest reasons that people are not interested in Christianity is because they think it is archaic. What does a book written thousands of years ago about a man who lived thousands of years ago, have to do with my needs today?

Good question! I hope you realize that the Christian has a good answer. The Word of God endures forever. The principles Christ taught and exemplified transcend time. They still work today.

Do you want to stay clear of AIDS or other sexually transmitted diseases? Then follow God's plan and be faithful in the marriage relationship (Proverbs 5:15).

Do you want a life of balance? Then take God at His Word when He promises a peace that passes understanding (Philippians 4:7).

Do you want to have a healthy self-image? Then believe that you were created in the image of God and that you are not here by accident, the mere result of a cosmic explosion (Genesis 1:27).

Do you want to be respected in the business world? Then protect your reputation through integrity and honesty (Proverbs 22:1).

And the list could go on and on and on and . . .

Confusing Methods

This was another method Christ intentionally used at times. The majority of Christ's teaching was done through parables, earthly stories with heavenly meaning. On the surface the purpose was hard to determine, but when thoroughly examined, the listeners found that God was teaching them some spiritual truth.

Last December my wife and I were watching the news when the weatherman gave an unseasonably warm forecast for Saturday. He said that the temperature on Saturday was going to be in the 60s. My wife looked at me and said, "Are you thinking what I'm thinking?" I said, "Does it start with a G?" Beth said, "Yes." And I said, "YES!" And she said, "Dave, I've never seen you so excited about cleaning the gutters!" I said, "Gutters. I was talking Golf!"

At times we communicate on different wave lengths. We find it easy to imitate Christ when it comes to confusing others with the gospel! We can confuse the issue and lose our listeners. Before you are too hard on yourself, remember, the Lord and his disciples were often on different wave lengths, too.

In Matthew 13 the disciples came to Jesus and wanted to know why He was always teaching in parables. He replied, "The knowledge of the secrets of the kingdom of heaven has been given to you, but not to them. . . . This is why I speak to them in parables: 'Though seeing, they do not see; though hearing, they do not hear or understand'" (Matthew 13:11,13).

Although it seemed confusing, it was effective in reaching many and causing people to ponder His words long after hearing them.

Clear Methods

Jesus was the Master when it came to preaching the good news of salvation to people. His words were practical and easy-to-follow. He used common illustrations and analogies that they could relate to. He didn't bore His listeners, and He knew when to quit.

Maybe you heard of the minister who just loved hearing the sound of his own voice. He thought he could wax eloquent for an eternity, and he did his best to try. One Sunday he kept preaching on and on. Finally, after a couple of hours a man got up and started walking out of the sanctuary.

The preacher yelled, "Hey, where are you going?" The man replied, "To get a haircut." The offended preacher yelled, "Why didn't you get one before you came to church?" The man hollered back, "I didn't need one then."

I hope that is not typical of your experience last Sunday. "We've a story to tell to the nations that will turn their hearts unto God." Our message, very simply, is Jesus Christ.

On one occasion Christ's followers expressed gratitude for His clarity.

> Then Jesus' disciples said, "Now you are speaking clearly and without figures of speech. Now we can see that you know all things and that you do not even need to have anyone ask you questions. This makes us believe that you came from God" (John 16:29,30).

At times, Jesus' teachings were easy to understand. If you think about some of your Christian friends you would say that some are more gifted to reach groups and crowds for Christ, while others have the ability to really impact individuals, one at a time. Jesus was the complete communicator: He knew how to reach the multitudes and how to relate one-on-one with a person. Whether you are sharing the gospel with one or one thousand what matters most is that the message is practical and understandable.

When people tell me that I have played some role in their conversion, they seldom talk about a particular sermon series, or a group of lessons I taught. But sometimes they will mention a simple illustration, a phrase, or an analogy that helped them understand a complex theological issue.

In fact, Christ's most familiar discourse, the Sermon on the Mount, was simple, basic, easy-to-follow conversational teaching. Fancy vocabulary and complex theology turn most people off. Their souls are not fed by "church talk." Dr. Karl Barth was once asked, "What is the deepest spiritual thought you have ever had?" He thought for a minute and then said, "Jesus loves me this I know, for the Bible tells me so."

Convicting Methods

Some people think that every sermon you hear is supposed to make you feel really good about yourself. But those individuals probably aren't looking for biblical preaching, for the Bible paints a different picture. At different times Christians need different admonitions. If sermons merely candy-coat Christianity, then we have avoided some of the main biblical purposes for preaching.

The apostle Paul says, "Preach the Word; be prepared in season and out of season; correct, rebuke and encourage — with great patience and careful instruction" (2 Timothy 4:2). Sometimes preaching is to convict, other times to instruct, its not always going to put you on a spiritual high!

It's like the church that got a new minister, and after his first sermon a member said, "It felt good to have my toes stepped on."

And the new minister said, "Didn't the last preacher step on your toes some?" The guy said, "Oh, yes, but there

63

was a difference. He seemed to enjoy doing it."

Sharing the gospel shouldn't come from a holier-than-thou attitude, or a condemning or judgmental spirit. Jesus balanced truth with tolerance. His message was convicting while not causing you to want to hide from God.

For some in His hometown of Nazareth, it was *too* convicting. On one occasion early in Christ's ministry, He read from the Old Testament in the synagogue. Then, in so many words, He told them that He had just fulfilled a Messianic prophecy and they had to accept Him on His terms. Guess how the people reacted?

> All the people in the synagogue were furious when they heard this. They got up, drove him out of the town, and took him to the brow of the hill on which the town was built, in order to throw him down the cliff (Luke 4:28,29).

It seems that Jesus was a huge hit everywhere except in His hometown, and with everyone except the religious leaders. They despised Him. The ones who had been charting the coming of the Messiah were the very ones who plotted to kill Him. They were enraged that Jesus preached and publicly exposed them for their arrogance and hypocrisy (Matthew 23). The people He came to save responded to His message, but the "spiritual leaders of the day" — well, that was a different story.

Recently I had the opportunity to speak before 2,000 freshmen at a large university in Texas. Since it was a church-related institution, they have a mandatory chapel/forum twice a week. I wasn't sure what to talk on, but I prepared, I prayed, I ran my ideas past those who invited me and then I did the best I could with my limited talent. To be honest, I thought it went well.

I found out the next week that the students enjoyed it and the administrators appreciated it, but I probably won't be invited back. Do you know why? Because one person didn't like the fact that I talked about heaven and hell. He said my talk was too evangelistic, and too convicting. Do you know who that one person was? The *chaplain* of the university. "Too evangelistic."

In those settings small or large, where you choose to share the good news, don't expect everyone to immediately embrace the gospel message — it won't happen. But neither should we think that God isn't big enough or the message of salvation isn't potent enough to overcome any obstacle — whether it's a crowd that wants to throw a preacher off a cliff or a chaplain who wants to silence a preacher from sharing the gospel, truth will prevail!

Compassionate Methods

Jesus said,

"A new command I give you: Love one another. As I have loved you, so you must love one another. By this all men will know that you are my disciples, if you love one another" (John 13:34,35).

Christ's sharing of the gospel was characterized by acts of compassion. (Not a bad step for laying the foundation in your evangelistic efforts.) Regardless of the setting, when children tried to sit on His lap, Jesus said, "Let the little children come unto me." The social outcasts of the day, lepers, the demon possessed — they all were touched physically, and spiritually, by Christ.

His love was evident when encountering the dishonest, (tax collectors), the outcast (lepers), the violent (demon possessed), the immoral (prostitutes), the wealthy (rich young ruler), and the poor (the widow with two mites).

What an example for us! Jesus rubbed shoulders with all segments of society. If we only reach out to those who come visit the church, then we have abandoned compassion and embraced convenience.

Do you remember the account in John 8, when Jesus delivered an extemporaneous sermon for a crowd of men who brought with them a woman caught in the act of adultery?

The compassion of Christ came through as He asked her,

> "Woman, where are they? Has no one condemned you?"
> "No one, sir," she said. "Then neither do I condemn you,"
> Jesus declared (John 8:10-11).

He maintained His love to her by not condemning her. But neither did He dilute the gospel. Listen to what He told her: "Go now, and leave your life of sin."

I talked to a guy recently who told me that his friend confided in him that he was having an affair. I said, "What did you say to him?" My friend said, "Well, at first I was tempted to say, I can kind of understand. Your wife has made your marriage miserable, and I know that the pressures are tough." But then he said, "As a Christian giving advice, I couldn't say that. So I told him he needed to stop that, repent before God, and work his hardest to try and reconcile his relationship with his wife."

He said it firmly, but he said it lovingly. When trying to impact people with the gospel, there's a real temptation to just excuse sin away. We can explain it as just being a result of how bad our culture has become. There is a temptation never to convict, rebuke, or challenge to change.

When Jesus spoke to this adulterous woman He didn't say, "Well, nowadays I can understand a little immorality. It's tough to be pure." He didn't say, "Try to cut back on the number of affairs you have each year, and in a few years you'll be faithful in a monogamous relationship."

No, Jesus compassionately preached the truth. The message He would have you convey is, "Repent, change, flee from this area of weakness, and don't do it again. Put your trust in the Spirit rather than in the flesh. The Holy Spirit can empower you to overcome it."

Christ in His wisdom employed a variety of ways of

sharing the gospel, because there are a variety of needs out there. It takes various methods and a variety of seeds to be planted before a crop can be harvested.

Over a decade ago, when I was a youth minister at the Shively Christian Church in Louisville, there was a young girl who started hanging around the Family Life Center. She had a terrible homelife. Her parents wouldn't drive her to church, but Tracy had a bike. Since she lived only a mile away from the church, she would ride her bike over. It became her escape. She played on a basketball team; she went to every youth activity. In reality, Tracy kind of became a project for the church, and the people fell in love with her.

After about two years, one Sunday night I had preached and offered an invitation. While we were singing, Tracy came forward to give her life to Christ. I had her repeat the good confession and then I said to the congregation of 200 people, "I'd like to do something I've never done before. If you have ever served as a youth sponsor for Tracy , or served as her basketball coach, if you've run the scoreboard, helped out on a youth retreat, taught Tracy in Sunday school, if you have ever had her in your home for a meal, or if you have ever prayed specifically for this girl — would you please stand up."

Over 100 people stood up. Although I was visibly moved, I was able to mumble, "That's the body of Christ, and that's what the apostle Paul meant when he said, 'I planted the seed, Apollos watered it, but God made it grow' (1 Corinthians 3:6)." You are called to plant seeds. Love is the soil of evangelism. At a Men's Retreat, Cal Thomas said, "Love talked about is easily ignored, but love demonstrated is irresistible."

Rarely does someone say, "You know, I just finished reading my New Testament, and I think I'm ready to become a Christian." They want to measure the authenticity of the gospel against the actual lifestyle of some

Christian. They want to see a sermon that matches the one they hear.

The Bottom Line

Stephen Olford said, "Jesus transformed a mountainside into a Bible conference; a fishing boat into an evangelistic platform; a well into a counseling room; and, the shadows of evening into an opportunity to lead Nicodemus into the experience of the new birth. He preached the Word continuously and so must we."

Regardless of the various places and methods, the main thing is to look for opportunities and to plant seeds. That's the best definition of sharing the gospel — planting seeds. Sometimes they will fall on fertile soil, at other times they won't. When it came to reaching out to the lost, Jesus "redeemed the time." When it comes to sharing your faith, are you making the most of the opportunities that God has afforded to you?

Although you may use different methods, remember you can't force your friends onto the pathway to Heaven, but you can lovingly lead them.

A Strategy for
Winning the Lost

Each year there are around 5,000 new companies started. Of those 5,000 only about 20% of them are still around one year later. Of those one thousand that survive only two hundred will celebrate their fifth anniversary. Most corporate consultants say there is a common denominator among those who fail: their organizations do not have a clear purpose. They lack a specific goal and direction.

Several years ago I walked into a popular fast food restaurant. (The month before I had spoken for the executives at the corporate headquarters of the food chain. My topic had been their mission statement and their promise.) As I walked to the counter I noticed the employee was wearing a button which said, "Committed to Our Promise." Being the cynical guy that I am I said, "I see your button, what's your promise?"

And that young girl began to rattle off each of the six prongs of their promise. It was incredible! She didn't miss a one. I was so dumbfounded that I thanked her and then kind of mumbled through an inarticulate order of chicken. You can understand why I was thrown off. I was amazed that a slogan which had been tossed around in some high level board meeting had made it through the ranks and been embraced by a minimum wage worker. It was impressive.

Jesus shared His mission statement in Luke 19:10. It was right after his transforming encounter with a greedy, dishonest tax collector named Zacchaeus. Jesus said, "The son of man has come to seek and save the lost."

The question is, some two thousand years later, is the mission still being embraced by His followers, or was it merely a catchy slogan from a messiah-wannabe?

When I was a student in Bible college one of the first things Professor Tom Thurman had the freshmen do was to memorize a definition of evangelism. It said, "Evangelism is the sharing of the good news with the lost with the intent of converting them to Christ, and the further sharing of the gospel with the saved, with the intent of conserving them for Christ." That is the purpose of the church and thus the purpose of each Christian. Are you committed to that promise?

In Acts 26 we are provided with a dramatic moment in the life of the apostle Paul. He'd been imprisoned for two years for sharing his faith. About that time Governor Festus (no relation to the Festus on "Gunsmoke") received word from the monarch, King Agrippa, that he was coming for a visit.

When he arrived, Festus, being aware that King Agrippa was intrigued by what he'd heard of Paul and Christianity, arranged a meeting with Paul. This way the governor could get the king's impression of the situation. What transpires is a Christian prisoner face to face with the most influential man around. But instead of using it as an opportunity to plead his own case he uses his time to try and witness on behalf of Christ.

The chapter provides you with a strategy for sharing your faith. There seem to be three different components of Paul's effort to evangelize. First he realized that he must . . .

Break Down Barriers

Paul has just witnessed a great parade and the entrance of the king, and so he joins right in with the mood that has been set through the pomp and ceremony. He begins by stating how lucky he is to stand before the king. He compliments the king's knowledge of the Jewish law. He proves himself and establishes credibility. Paul even skillfully places King Agrippa and himself in the same boat of people who have been anxiously awaiting the promised Messiah. This is not false flattery — it is building rapport and bringing down the defenses.

Few people become Christians through door-to-door evangelism, or an abrupt heavy-duty guilt trip. Decisions for Christ usually require quantities of time; times of getting better acquainted, establishing credibility and trust so that people feel comfortable and are open to what you have to say.

Several years ago our Insurance Agent called and said that he wanted to talk to my wife and me. (Translated that means that he wanted to sell us more insurance.) The night before his visit, Beth and I prepared by asking each other mock questions. We felt that we could combat any tactic he might employ. Our minds were made up — No More Insurance.

The next day the meeting began with small talk and common interests. It seemed to be going well. Gradually he steered the conversation toward insurance. When he seemed to be trying to get us to buy more insurance we rattled off one of our rehearsed responses. After about 45 minutes the meeting was wrapping up when he said, "Dave, if you were to die Beth only has enough life insurance to cover her for about five years. What happens after that?"

(No sweat, we had anticipated this question.) I answered, "We've talked about that and since Beth is young we feel that she would probably remarry within five years."

My agent kind of paused and cocked his head to the side and said, "Yeah, maybe, maybe so Dave, but that guy has got some awfully big shoes to fill."

I had never thought of that. And then he said, "I doubt if she could find another Dave Stone in five years time."

To make a long story short I bought a million dollar policy! (Well it wasn't quite that much, but it was more than I intended.) It would be an understatement to say that my insurance agent knew how to break down barriers.

Jesus was a master at that. Acts 26 shows us that the apostle Paul wasn't too shabby himself. Here is this prisoner, face to face with the king and he is somehow able to work his way into talking about the spiritual issues of life which will affect eternity.

How do you break down barriers? (Doing lunch, a sporting event, an invitation to your church on Friend Sunday or at Easter, an afternoon of shopping together, a ticket to a Christmas pageant at church, a sermon tape from a message from your minister you think they may enjoy, a round of golf together, a Christian book on a topic of interest, the list goes on and on . . .)

Several years ago our church invited Bill Hybels to speak at Southeast. I remember him sharing a story with our leadership about a woman in their church. He said, "We used to have people who had joined Willow Creek stand up with the person who had invited them to start coming. Each month I kept seeing the same woman stand up with a different person who had joined. Finally one day I asked her about it, and this is the way she explained it.

"'I'm not gifted to teach, or to sing but I do feel comfortable inviting people to come to church with me, so I guess I'm a 'bringer.'"

Maybe you can't answer every theological question which arises from your friends. Maybe you don't feel that

God has blessed you with "public gifts" that can reach the masses. But just maybe God desires you to help in another way, as a "bringer." It starts with breaking down barriers, it continues when you . . .

Focus on the Facts

After Paul gets the attention of the crowd he wastes no time in moving onto the next phase of his discourse. The facts that he centers upon are his own life and the life of Christ. Throughout the book of Acts repeatedly Paul shares his personal testimony. There is a reason for that, and a lesson for each Christian to learn. If you give an argument on behalf of the Bible or the Lord someone will always have a counter argument. But if you give your personal testimony it's irrefutable. People can believe or disbelieve personal experiences but they cannot be refuted.

But then Paul turns the attention to where he really wants it to be — on Jesus, and the fact that He has conquered death. Paul says, "But I have had God's help to this very day, and so I stand here and testify to small and great alike. I am saying nothing beyond what the prophets and Moses said would happen — that the Christ would suffer and, as the first to rise from the dead, would proclaim light to his own people and to the Gentiles" (Acts 26:22-23).

Christianity rises or falls upon the resurrection of Jesus Christ. It is the only religion that claims to have a leader whom death could not keep. The reality of the resurrection sparks hope within every believer. If Christ conquered the grave, then so can Christians.

Paul's audience is quite aware of the Old Testament prophecies concerning the Messiah and the allusions to a bodily resurrection. Paul is merely focusing on the facts in an effort to put the pieces of the puzzle together for them. His task is to proclaim to them that their waiting for the

Messiah is over, for it is Jesus who fulfilled all of those prophecies.

As Paul tries to challenge his listeners to become Christians, he sets for you and me an example to keep "the main thing, the main thing."

Perhaps you have heard about the problem they had in London a number of years ago. They had buses driving right past their customers. The passengers were at the proper place at the proper time but the buses went sailing right past them. To explain their actions, the London Transit Authorities released a statement which has become infamous with public relations departments everywhere. It read: "It is impossible for us to maintain our schedules if we are always having to stop and pick up passengers."

Gee, I thought that was the reason we have buses, you know, to give people rides. The reason we have churches is to reach the lost, to give them hope, to replace frowns with smiles because of the reality of a risen Savior.

Our Music Minister, Dale Mowery, attended a conference last year in which he was able to hear a top executive from Disneyworld. The man related how several years ago through exit surveys they found that some families were leaving the theme park disappointed. They had come to see someone, but during their visit they never crossed paths with him. His name was Mickey Mouse.

But the Disney executives are in the business of giving people what they want, so they created a way for everyone who wanted to see Mickey to be able to see Mickey. Now, at noon, on any day of the week a parade comes down Main Street with you-know-who leading the way. The result? Children now leave the park happy and content because of whom they saw.

It's important to remember that illustration for the Disney discovery applies to the church as well. People come to church because they want to see someone. His name is Jesus. He can meet their needs and save their souls. Whenever you find yourself with an opportunity to share your faith, remember where the focus needs to be. People desperately want and need to see Jesus. Don't disappoint them.

The final step in Paul's strategy was to . . .

Request a Response

Maybe you have a hard time challenging people to a deeper level of commitment. Christians have a tendency to clam up when it comes to the influential or powerful. And yet Christians should not be intimidated to share the gospel with today's version of King Agrippa (the CEO, the wealthy, the professional athlete, the television personality).

It seems that monthly I am interviewed by a television reporter concerning something that our church is involved in. Every time after the interview I invite them to come and visit a worship service at Southeast. The next day I send the reporter and the camera person a thank you note and some literature on the church. The day after that I ask another person from their same station to try and invite them to come. If the reporter is a lady then my wife sometimes calls and offers to sit with them in a service.

The more soft touches from caring people, the better the chance we have of their coming to hear the gospel. Several years ago I decided that I can either use the pulpit to take shots at the "media" or I can use some of my time to befriend the media and encourage them and try to model Christlike behavior. Amazingly many have taken me up on the invitation and visited. Some of them have become very dear friends.

Often times Christians breeze through the first two steps. Making small talk and finding common ground isn't burdensome. In fact if you enjoy the person's company breaking down barriers is nothing more than building a friendship. Focusing on the facts is a little tougher but to some requesting a response borders on fanaticism. It's one thing to invite someone to church; it's another thing to challenge a person to surrender to the Lordship of Jesus Christ.

How many times have you prayed for an "open door" to witness, only to close it fearfully in the face of someone who needs Christ? It's like the salesman who doesn't have the courage to say, "Those are the facts about the product — what do you think?" It's like the hunter who sees the game but can't pull the trigger.

You will never win anyone to Christ if you never try. This sounds basic, but Christians often neglect it. Paul's love for the lost was evidently greater than his fear of ridicule or rejection.

Then Paul says, "King Agrippa, do you believe the prophets? I know you do" (Acts 26:27).

Paul puts Agrippa on the hot seat, "Do you believe the prophets?" If Agrippa says no, he will alienate the Jewish nation he is trying to govern. If the king says yes, he will be put in a vulnerable position to accept the Messiah who has fulfilled the prophecies of centuries. So he tries to escape with sarcasm.

Then Agrippa says to Paul, "Do you think that in such a short time you can persuade me to be a Christian?"

Paul replies, "Short time or long — I pray God that not only you but all who are listening to me today may become what I am, except for these chains" (Acts 26:28-29).

Paul is a prisoner, in chains for Christ, and how he takes advantage of his adversity! Instead of looking at this speech as a ticket to freedom he views it as an opportunity to preach Christ to the king and to an enlightened audience of the movers and shakers of his time.

It would have been very easy for Paul to deliver an eloquent speech which would get his chains removed. There's a simple explanation for why he shared what he did. Paul was more concerned about others' salvation than his freedom.

I've heard Bob Russell talk about Hide-n-Seek being one of his favorite games as a child. You would get a good hiding place and as you stay contorted in some strange location you say, "They'll never find me here!" But the longer you hide there, and the more people are too scared even to move into your area, the more frightened you become.

And while your words haven't changed, your tone has, as you fearfully say, "They'll never find me here." So what do you do? You cough, or break a branch or stick out a leg — anything to attract the attention of the others. Then when they follow the obvious noises, and come to you, you say, "Aw, shucks you found me!" The truth of the matter is you wanted to be found.

Somehow when you go to work or you move within your circle of acquaintances or you find yourself at some party, try to see things through spiritual eyes. If you're perceptive, through spiritual ears, you just may hear a lost person cough, or break a branch. It might be in the form of a question about your positive attitude, or it could be through some gentle kidding about your lifestyle. Regardless of the way they choose to send up the red flag, be on the lookout for the lost and help them find the way. If you're a Christian who is "committed to our promise" then you'll do it.

There are masses of people who need Jesus and you can help reach them, one at a time. Did you notice that I chose to do this chapter on an encounter which seemingly failed to win a lost king? It's no accident I chose this story, for you must remember it is not our responsibility to "make them grow" or "give the increase." That is God's job. We've talked about it before — our task is not to personally save people but to plant seeds and introduce them to Jesus.

In the Gospels, Jesus condemned a fig tree. It is important to realize why He did that. Jesus didn't condemn the fig tree because it was old, or because it was gnarled. Christ condemned the fig tree because it didn't bear fruit. The message is obvious: God wants us to reproduce ourselves in the lives of others. The church is the only organization which exists for those people who are not yet members.

The Bottom Line

Rick Rusaw is a good friend of mine who preaches at a church in Longmont, Colorado. Recently Rick told me of something which happened to him while attending a Promise Keepers Conference in Denver.

He told me that a national television news program had been in and out of sessions gathering footage for an upcoming program. At one point the crowd began singing "Amazing Grace." Rick said, "Here were 70,000 men in Mile High Stadium singing the story of their lives. Everyone could sense that this was special. But about that time, Maria Shriver came walking in with her camera crew and instantly they realized that this was the footage they desperately needed."

Rick said, "The crew took off running for the front of the stadium so that they could get a shot of all these men singing 'Amazing Grace.'" As Shriver passed Rick, he heard her say to her camera man, "If we don't get this, we're dead."

The next week Rick told his congregation, "I don't know what their boss would do to them if they missed out on getting that footage. But I do know that if we don't get God's amazing grace, we're dead!"

Hebrews 2:3 says, "How shall we escape if we ignore such a great salvation?"

Paul had a strategy for reaching the lost. He was committed to his promise to reach them. Paul broke down barriers, focused on the facts, and requested a response. How about you? When it comes to reaching the lost with the gospel, you can build a bridge or you can build a wall. The choice is yours.

Becoming All Things, to All People

Christians must be good news before they can take the good news. One of the reasons that Jesus experienced such success in His outreach was His ability to relate to people. He knew how to meet their needs and touch their hearts. In this chapter the focus will be different ways that Christians can enhance their crediblity with the lost in order to positively influence the world for Jesus.

Be Prayerful

Let me encourage you to make a list of people whom you want to influence for Christ. Remember that old cliche: He who fails to plan, plans to fail. The same is true when it comes to sharing your faith. God is the one who is able to work in the lives of those you are trying to reach. He needs to be part of your plan.

Your list will be a combination of people from different groups. It may include unsaved family members, co-workers, neighbors and acquaintances with whom you cross paths on a regular basis. Begin to pray for the people on your list. If you are married, each night as a couple you may choose to pray specifically for another couple on your list. Pray that God will soften their hearts and that the seeds you plant will find fertile soil.

Jesus said, "Ask and it will be given to you" (Matthew 6:7a). If winning the lost is really important to you, then it can become very natural for you to pray regularly for loved ones and acquaintances who need Christ.

Be Realistic

You can't win everyone to the Lord. In Mark 10 when Jesus, the master evangelist challenged the rich young ruler to follow Him, the ruler walked away in sadness. The cost of discipleship was too high. At different seasons of life, depending upon their circumstances, people may be more hardened or more open to the gospel. Your job is to plant seeds realizing that God gives the increase.

If your expectations are unrealistic they will lead to disappointment. God hasn't called you to single-handedly win the world, but He has commissioned you to share the gospel "as you are going."

Years ago I read a great story in a church newsletter. It told of an older gentleman walking the beach at dawn who noticed a young man ahead of him, picking up starfish and flinging them into the sea. The older man caught up with him and asked the youth what he was doing.

The answer was that the stranded starfish would die if left until the morning sun. The older man said, "Yes, but the beach goes on for miles, and there are millions of starfish. How can your effort make any difference?"

The young man looked at the starfish in his hand and as he threw it to safety in the waves he said, "It makes a difference to this one."

You do your best to be a faithful witness of the difference Christ has made in your life. That is all the Lord is asking and that is all He expects of you in your evangelistic endeavors. So stop allowing Satan to put you on a guilt trip for wasted chances in the past. Instead set your sights on the future opportunities which God will avail to you.

Be Servant-Minded

In my first ministry I worked at another church in Louisville, the Shively Christian Church, where I served as the youth minister. One summer Wednesday night my lesson for the teens was on servanthood (Jesus washing the feet of the disciples). To make the lesson stick, I divided all thirty-five kids into groups and said, "For the next two hours I want you to go out and be Jesus to the city of Louisville. If Jesus were here in the flesh where would He go, what would He do, whom would He serve? We'll meet back at my apartment in two hours and share our stories."

They dived into cars and headed out. Upon their return there was a lot of excitement. We packed my apartment and started listening to each group tell of their attempts to be like Jesus through their service. One group told of pooling their money together and buying ice cream cones and delivering them to some widow ladies in a nearby apartment complex. Another group went to a hospital, bought a get well card, and visited with a man from church.

Part of my gang included two seventh grade boys who felt that they had a brilliant idea. They wanted to go to a gas station and pump gas for people so the customers wouldn't even have to get out of their car. I quickly nixed that based upon a mathematical equation: Seventh graders + Gasoline = Trouble. The next day's headlines might say, "Seventh Graders Posing as Jesus, Blow Up City." Instead we did some yard work for a man.

Another group went to a nursing home and sang Christmas carols. (Now you've got to remember this was in August!) We later found out that the residents enjoyed it, but it was a little confusing to some of them! ("Maude, this is the hottest Christmas I can remember.")

About that time another group came straggling in to

my apartment. I said, "Where have you all been? You're late."

Greg, their teenage driver, spoke up and said, "When we left the Shively Christian parking lot, we went over to Shively Baptist." (Everybody kind of went, "Ooohh," because they were our archrivals in church softball and basketball.)

Greg continued, "The preacher told us that there was an elderly lady from their church who needed some yard work done, but they hadn't been able to get anybody to do it, so we volunteered. We drove over there and mowed and raked and trimmed. When we were loading up to leave she came over to thank us and she said, 'Thank you so much. You kids at Shively Baptist are always coming to my rescue!'"

And I interrupted him and said, "Well Greg, didn't you tell her you were from Shively Christian?"

And Greg said, "No, I really didn't think it mattered."

He was right. It didn't matter and it doesn't matter. If you really want to serve as the Lord did and impact people the way Christ did, then you're really not obsessed with which church or which individual gets the pat on the back. Jesus said, "Let your light shine before men, that they may see your good deeds and praise your Father in heaven" (Matthew 5:16). And what Jesus told you to do is exactly what the world is waiting to see: people who live the sermons they preach.

If you want to get the attention of the lost, then "wash feet" and surprise them with your service. It is a way to lovingly lead the lost to the Lord. That is precisely the "how" and "why" that Christ came. As He put it, "For even the Son of Man did not come to be served, but to serve, and to give his life as a ransom for many" (Mark 10:45).

Be Flexible

Several years ago my preacher friend Wayne Smith told me of going out to speak at the Central Christian Church in Las Vegas. It is one of the fastest growing churches in the country. They have had great success at reaching the unchurched with the gospel. Being from the "old school" Wayne noticed that there were no hymns in the worship service.

That afternoon the former president of the University of Nevada-Las Vegas gave Wayne a ride to the airport. Since they were about the same age Wayne asked him, "Do you enjoy singing all these new worship choruses?"

The man was quite candid with his reply. He said, "No — but we sure are winning a lot of people!"

The apostle Paul had the right attitude when he said, "To the weak I became weak, to win the weak. I have become all things to all men so that by all possible means I might save some" (1 Corinthians 9:22).

Be Creative

Jesus maintained his message, but He often creatively reached out to people. To the Samaritan woman He asked questions. It was unheard of in Christ's day for a man to speak to a woman in public, especially for a Jew to speak to a Samaritan. But that was just another expression of His creative attempts to scratch where people itched.

The church where I serve, Southeast Christian, has some really creative soul winners. For the past seven years we have added over 1,000 new members each year. What a testimony to the commitment of our membership! They love to tell others about their church and about their Lord.

One doctor sometimes writes a prescription to patients which says: Try Southeast once a weekend for one month, then call me in the morning.

A former elder sometimes challenges co-workers to come for four straight weekends. His rationale is that they can make a discerning decision after being exposed to both of us who preach, and hearing the different styles of special music and congregational singing. He also knows that by coming for a month the visitor can get a more balanced feel for the friendliness and the mission of the church.

Another person says to people, "Come with me to church, and if you don't like it I'll buy you a steak dinner for lunch." (He often asks what weekends I am scheduled to preach. I'm not sure whether that is a compliment or a means of saving money!)

Due to the crowded conditions at Southeast, the traffic can be a real nightmare. One couple shared with a group of us that the first time they visited Southeast, they didn't mean to. They were driving to their church trying to get over into another lane. The only problem was they got caught in the flow of traffic coming to Southeast and the police officer directing traffic wouldn't allow them to change lanes. So reluctantly the couple pulled in and parked their car. They came on in to see what it was like, and several months later they parked their membership at Southeast.

Even our traffic jams can be a method of evangelism. That is being creative. Most churches have a calling program — we just have four police officers who love to point people in the right direction!

Two years ago my dentist was flying back to Louisville and he struck up a conversation with his seat-mate who had just moved to Louisville. Since the man's wife and family wouldn't be able to move for another month Carl invited him over to dinner the same night that some of the church staff were going to be there. Things went well that night. Bill visited church (he hadn't been to one in over ten years). He and his family now come regularly and are growing in the Lord, all because 30,000 feet in the air a dentist invited a lonely newcomer to dinner before inviting him to church.

The possibilities are endless when it comes to creative ways you can reach people for Christ. Let your imagination run wild.

Be a Friend

Be aware that when you help to take a person to a deeper level in their walk with Christ you will need to continue to help them grow spiritually. Too many new converts have faded fast from the faith due to being abandoned by the ones who were instrumental in leading them to Christ. Baby Christians need attention, accountability and above all else encouragement. In business if you work for months to hire an executive you spend the next few months helping that person make the transition in their new setting. The business world calls that "protecting your investment." Christians must do the same.

One reason that some slip back into their previous lifestyle is because they are not willing to form some new friendships and sever some of their old ones. The well-intentioned new Christian may be duped by the devil into thinking that when it comes to unchristian friendships he is bringing them *up* when in reality they are bringing him *down*.

I had a good friend tell me he stopped playing golf because when he golfed with his buddies inevitably he would return to his drinking, smoking and cussing. And he didn't like the person he was becoming.

I told him that while I was proud of him, he really didn't need to quit golfing — he just needed some new golfing buddies who shared the same priorities and commitment to Christ. So now he golfs with me and he's doing great! (The bad news is now I've started drinking, smoking and cussing! Not really, but if any sport could drive me to it, it would be golf.)

Forming a strong Christian friendship merely solidifies the commitment that was made and speeds up the maturing process. It communicates to the one you have reached out to, "You are not in this alone; I'm here to help you."

Be Joyful

Christians should be the happiest people in the world and that attribute should spill over into your witnessing. Let people know that they can face life or death with assurance and confidence if they are in Christ. The reality of that truth should make both of you joyful!

Bob Russell tells me that years ago George Brown, who is now a member of our church, struggled with Christianity. Could he believe the gospel even later in life? When he was in his fifties he accepted Christ and was baptized. One of the factors that helped convince him of the truth of the gospel was his job. George worked as a manager of Cave Hill Cemetery.

Every week George saw scores of people lay their loved ones to rest. After working there for some time he said, "I've noticed a profound difference between the way Christians mourn for their loved ones, and the way the non-Christians mourn."

The apostle Paul said, "Brothers, we do not want you to be ignorant about those who fall asleep, or to grieve like the rest of men, who have no hope" (1 Thessalonians 4:13).

Beneath the pain Christians have a joy that the world can't take away because "This world is not my home, I'm just a passin' through." Paul could write from a prison cell that he had learned to be content, whether in plenty or in need, because he was joyful that he had the assurance of salvation.

This book is unusual. It is rare that an author's first

book is dedicated to his mother-in-law. But if you would have known my mother-in-law then it wouldn't seem unusual. Through her life, so many people from all walks of life "saw a sermon."

In the last month of writing this book Bette Bowman died after battling cancer for eighteen months. She was only 53 years old. Her life was an awesome example to me. Bette was a committed Christian who even in the midst of tremendous pain and adversity maintained a positive spirit. She suffered through a mastectomy, chemotherapy, losing her hair on two different occasions, radiation and more chemotherapy. But through it all she remained joyful. Bette accepted her dying as an opportunity to influence others for Christ.

The last four days of her life all five of her kids and their spouses were constantly by her bedside. We sang worship choruses and her favorite hymns. We also did a lot of weeping and waiting.

But I want to tell you about the last few hours of Bette Bowman's life. At one in the morning each family member and their spouse came past and said their name in her ear and whispered some final words. And then I said, "Bette, there is a downside to having a daughter who marries a preacher. You're going to have to listen to your last sermon, and I'm going to preach it."

The impromptu sermon went through several passages in Revelation 21 and 22, which described what she was about to see and experience in heaven. And I talked about her new, glorified body that she would have. Our blood pumped faster as we became more and more excited for her with every verse.

Then my wife's brother Tommy, pulled out a guitar and played and sang a song that he had written the night before for his mother. As we dried our tears, we assured Bette that we would be okay, and that if Jesus was ready for her, then we could let go.

About a half hour after that, with her husband, sister, and every son and daughter kneeling around her bedside, she took her last breath. Her eyes started to open and then she died.

No more sporadic breathing, no more oxygen mask, no more pulsating chest, no more wig, no more prosthetic bra — just peace. For a couple of minutes there were tears and sobbing. But then something happened. It was incredible. In a matter of seconds the mood changed.

Bette's sister said, "Praise God."

I said, "Bette, you hung in there for this moment. You're home now."

Someone said, "Mom, you made it, you made it. Praise the Lord."

Her daughter Jill said, "Satan, you lost. You tried to wear her down with cancer, but you lost."

Someone else said, "Death, where is your sting?"

Then her son Tommy said, "Victory! Victory!"

And then Bette's son-in-law Paul said, "Victory in Jesus." He started singing the song, "Victory in Jesus," and everyone of us joined in tearfully singing through it.

The world can't understand that type of rationale, for to the world, death is defeat. But I can confidently say to you that when Bette Bowman and her cancer ridden body took her last breath — she had won. Because she had a personal relationship with Jesus Christ, in spite of our pain, the family can honestly say: "Victory. Victory. Victory in Jesus."

When you think about it, a person cannot die with that kind of assurance unless earlier in life someone had introduced them to Jesus Christ and that individual accepted Him. The joy comes from God's promise of eternal life. I don't know about you but that gets me pumped up and excited to share my faith.

The Bottom Line

Recently I was playing golf with a good friend. Throughout the day I had been trying to take advantage of opportunities to plant some seeds of faith in my caddy. On the back nine my friend Steve and I got to talking about some of the areas of his life in the past that he was trying to forsake. The caddy overheard our conversation and he said, "Sounds like hanging around with the preacher has changed your life a lot."

I loved Steve's reply. He said, "Yeah, he's helped out some, but he hasn't changed me — Jesus Christ has changed me."

It is so important to remember that when you share your faith, you are just an instrument, a vessel that God can use. Steve is right, Jesus Christ is the only one who has the power to transform lives. So try to become all things, to all people, so that by all possible means you can save some. The Lord only asks that you be ready and willing to share the good news. The rest is up to Him.

Reaching through Preaching

Stephen Brown, a popular radio minister, tells of being on a cross-country flight when an elderly man seated near him became ill. Despite attention from two doctors on board, the passenger died in mid-flight. Brown said an incredible hush came over the plane. The flight attendants covered the body with blankets and waited while the pilot made an emergency landing in Dallas. Everyone was ordered off the plane while the coroner removed the body.

When the passengers reboarded, Brown could feel the tension. So he said to the flight attendant, "Ma'am, I'm a minister. I've been around death a lot. If you'd like for me to say a few words or do something, I'll be glad to help."

She said, "Thanks, but we won't need you. We're just going to give free drinks to everyone on board."

The preacher and his message aren't very welcome in our society. With the information explosion and the multitude of self-help resources at our fingertips, preaching isn't all that popular.

In recent years, when it comes to respect and credibility, preachers have been slipping. The other day I saw a chain letter that has the potential of being quite hazardous to the health of your minister. It's for people who don't like their preacher. It says:

If you are not happy with your preacher then send this notice to six other churches that are tired of their preacher, too. Then bundle up your preacher and send him to the church at the top of your list. Within a week you will receive 1,643 preachers. One of them should be just right for your church's needs. Have faith in this letter, don't break it. One church in Wyoming broke the chain and they got their old preacher back!!!

Jesus Came to Preach

When Jesus preached, He touched a number of emotional chords in people. Some wanted to bundle Him up and throw Him off of a cliff. Others wanted to embrace Him and His message. Jesus had a gift at balancing truth and tolerance. He gave people direction in their lives so they would be able to find heaven.

Jesus stated a number of reasons for why He came to earth. On one occasion He said to his disciples, "Let us go somewhere else — to the nearby villages — so I can preach there also. That is why I have come" (Mark 1:38).

If preaching the gospel was such a high priority with Christ, it should be a high priority with us as well. You can learn a great deal about reaching the lost by studying the Master. Through His preaching we learn how to share the gospel.

The message that Christ preached could be summed up in one word — *hope*. He taught that you don't have to go to hell because of your sin; instead, if you put your trust in Him, and live for Him, you can have heaven. Every concern from the past and hope for the future were taken care of when God sent Jesus to earth.

The Bible tells us that at the age of thirty He began preaching. Although His ministry lasted only three years, it changed the world. Preaching about Him 2,000 years later still has the power to change the world.

But for that to happen, Christians must get involved in

proclaiming the good news. Jesus said to His disciples, "The harvest is plentiful but the workers are few. Ask the Lord of the harvest, therefore, to send out workers into his harvest field" (Matthew 9:37,38).

We Still Need Preachers to Share the Gospel

John Stott said, "Preaching is indispensable to Christianity." The world today may ridicule the message and the messenger who stands behind the pulpit, but the fact remains, God still uses preaching to communicate His Word with power.

Someone pointed out to me that nowhere in the Bible are we specifically commanded to pray for the lost, but in Matthew 9 we are commanded by Christ to pray for people to reach the lost. But in recent decades, as ministry has become more specialized, churches have gradually faded from challenging young men to consider becoming preachers.

When I was fifteen years old I made a commitment at a Christ in Youth Conference that I would go to Bible college and pursue some type of ministry. (This was deeper than my pledge to God from a wrestling mat in the eighth grade!) But in the middle of my senior year of high school I had to come face to face with following through on that decision. I started to waver. I had earned some scholarship money to Cincinnati Bible College by winning several state preaching contests, and as Senior Class President, when I gave the senior charge to the graduating class the principal was supposed to say what my college plans were.

One evening, several weeks before graduation, my mom and I got in a deep conversation. My father wasn't home at the time; he was preaching somewhere that night. I told my mother that I had narrowed my career goals to being a preacher, a radio DJ, a politician, or a comedian.

She said, "Your father wrestled with some of those things when he was deciding what to do." And she said, "Follow me." Mom went to her closet in their bedroom and had me pull down a big box. She showed me all of these different awards that my father won in high school. One year he was selected as one of two young men to represent New Mexico in Washington D.C. at Boys Nation.

She said, "Your dad, when he was a senior in high school, entered a speech contest, and he won for the city. Then he won for his county, and then subsequently he won the state."

I couldn't believe this. My father had never mentioned any of this to me! Then Mom pulled back another layer of cotton, revealing one more award and she said, "And then he won the grand diamond."

I asked, "What's the grand diamond?"

"That's when he advanced to the national speaking finals, and he won that, and he was named the best speaker in the country," she said proudly.

This was all news to me. So when my father got home that night, we looked through the box together. He told me that when he was a senior, his interests were similar to mine. He had his own Saturday morning radio program in Albuquerque, so he was interested in being a DJ, but he also had a real interest in politics, in journalism, and in preaching.

I asked, "Then how did you decide?"

He said, "I prayed about it a lot, and I knew that God could have used me in any of those areas. He needs strong Christians in those fields, but I thought and prayed, 'God, where could You use me the most?' And when it came down to that, I felt that He was calling me to attend a Christian college and to be open to His leading."

I'll never forget what he said to me next. "Dave, you know the amazing thing is, God is so good, that since deciding to go into the ministry, He's brought all of those other passions into my life," he said. (You see, my dad has preached on the radio several times over the years, and he currently serves as the editor of a Christian magazine, and several years ago he was sent to Poland to represent Americans who had helped them during their food crisis.)

That night I didn't sleep much, but I sure did pray. And it became very clear to me that God was calling me to attend Cincinnati Bible College and learn to preach the gospel, and for that to be my vocation.

God is so good. He's even allowed me to mesh my other passions in with this job. I'm able to speak and use humor in secular settings and still slide in a Christian message. I'm able to preach at the greatest church in the country.

As far as being a politician, I'm able to shake about 500 hands each weekend at my church. (And occasionally I even make promises that I know I can't keep!)

Paul said, "How, then, can they call on the one they have not believed in? And how can they believe in the one of whom they have not heard? And how can they hear without someone preaching to them? And how can they preach unless they are sent?" (Romans 10:14-15a).

Teenagers

If you are a teenager and you found this book in a dumpster while hiding from your principal, then please read this next paragraph.

I challenge you to consider saying "no" to the American dream and saying "yes" to God's will. I have never regretted my decision to go to a Bible college and to be open to ministry. If you feel that God is calling you to serve Him in a vocational way, then talk to someone about it, pray about it, and follow through.

Grandparents

If you are a grandparent, perhaps you can help with

your resources to send a grandchild to receive a Christian education. You might be in a financial position to do this at this stage of your life. Or maybe you could contact your minister and he could match you up with a deserving teenager who has a passion to share the gospel, but financially finds it impossible to go to college and study for the ministry.

Parents

If you are a parent, be aware that it's easy for God to tug at a teenager's heart. Sometimes it's tough for parents to willingly encourage and seek what God wants for their children's future. Sometimes Christian parents will say to their teen, "You are so intelligent; you have so many skills; I can't believe you're thinking about being a Christian school teacher, or a preacher, or a missionary."

True, your children might not live in the next subdivision and bring the grandchildren over each week for Sunday dinner. And they might not make as much money as you do. They might not attend your alma mater. But the truth of the matter is that they just might be fulfilled and happy in the ministry because they know they are doing what God has called them to do! Remember, the church is only one generation from extinction.

Church Members

Years ago, Lloyd Pelfrey, president of Central Christian College of the Bible, was attending an event for the alumni of the college. A preacher came up to him who had graduated a number of years before. He slapped the president on the back and said, "Well, President Pelfrey, are we graduating some *great* preachers this year?" The President was quite candid in his reply; he said, "If you want eagles, then you've got to send us eagle eggs!"

He's right. Don't expect quality leadership if you don't

care enough to send the best for Christian training. (My church is probably thinking: instead of an eagle, how'd we get stuck with a turkey? Well don't blame me, it's my home church's fault!) The Hallmark® Card Company says it well, "Care enough to send the very best." Within the church you can have a big influence on future Christian leaders. Pray for them. Encourage them. Plant the idea of ministry in their minds. When they participate in a worship service, make it a point to seek them out and tell them how proud you are that they are using their gifts for God's glory. Young people need to be challenged and inspired to serve in a big way, and they need to be open to God's calling.

In recent years Christian colleges have seen a real increase in the number of non-traditional students — people in their thirties and forties — who have felt unfulfilled in their chosen careers and feel a real passion for ministry. They have begun to pursue training for some type of Christian service, because they have a desire to share the gospel.

In case you are reading this chapter and you are thinking, "This doesn't pertain to me," let me share a concern that is even more important than attracting more people to be preachers.

We All Need to Share the Gospel

Jesus challenged His followers to do that. He said to them, "Go into all the world and preach the good news to all creation" (Mark 16:15). Let me remind you, if you have accepted Christ as your Lord and Savior, then you have already agreed to confess Him before others on an ongoing basis. It's more than just darkening the doorway of a church on weekends; it's a lifestyle.

In Mark 1:40-44 Jesus healed a man with leprosy and He told him not to tell anyone. Jesus knew that it was too early in His ministry for His travels to be impeded by the crowds. But here was this man, whose skin had been ravaged by leprosy. Now he was cleansed by Christ, and he was told not to tell a soul. Is it surprising that he went out and told everyone he knew?

I'm not condoning his disobedience. But this man was told to shut his mouth — we've been told to open ours! If our faith is real, then it will permeate our conversations. Rather than concealing our convictions and downplaying our devotion, as Christians we must speak a good word for Jesus. God places you in the pathway of people who are lost and desperately need to be found. With some, you may be *the only* person who can reach them.

Different methods reach people in different ways. You might reach someone by a strong confrontation of a questionable lifestyle, but more likely you will reach him by saying, "I'm praying for you during this tough time, and if you ever want to talk, I'm available."

Some will be reached by an excellent pageant at your church, but probably more will be reached by a small support group where they are surrounded by people with a common struggle. Some will be moved by a sermon from a teenager on a Youth Night; others will be reached by a guest speaker or the consistent preaching of the regular minister.

If the truth were known, most people respond to the gospel, not because of what a paid professional imparts from the pulpit. They respond to Christ because they see Christ fleshed out for them in the life of a Christian friend, neighbor, or boss. They would rather see our sermon than hear it. And when people see that distinctive difference, they can't help but be drawn in to find out more about Jesus.

Ben Merold says, "When the prodigal gets to the pig sty, he is looking for someone to show him the way home." Only eternity will be able to measure the good accomplished for the kingdom because Christians chose to share the gospel with non-Christians. But the converse is true as well.

The Bottom Line

Did you know that Gandhi almost became a Christian? He read the Bible from cover to cover. He studied the claims of Christianity. Gandhi even read the New Testament several times. But then do you know what happened? He visited the United States. This influential leader made a swing through the southern portion of our country where our Bible-believing churches are strongest, and the same thing happened at each town he visited. They would not let him in the restaurants because of the color of his skin.

Gandhi later wrote in his personal journal that he rejected Christianity, not because of Christ, but because of Christians. What an indictment against believers! Never underestimate the influence you can have, positive or negative, by the life that you live. Preaching is more than proclaiming, it's living.

Last December I did something I hate to do. I made my annual pilgrimage to the attic to bring down countless boxes of Christmas decorations. This is a real big deal for our kids. It was about four years ago that my wife, Beth, ordered a baby Jesus doll that is actually the size of a baby. Now each December the children enjoy opening the boxes and finding the baby Jesus. When they find Him, they spend most of the month of December taking turns holding Jesus and talking to Him.

Later that night I came into the living room and my daughter Sadie, who was three at the time, was sitting on the floor next to Samuel, her nine-month-old brother. Sadie was holding the baby Jesus. She placed Him in Samuel's lap and said, "Now, Jesus, this is Samuel; and, Samuel, this is Jesus."

101

Let me ask you something. When was the last time you introduced someone to Jesus? Not through a sermon — but through your lifestyle, not from a pulpit but on a tennis court or across a restaurant table.

The Motivation:

Salvation to Be Shared

Forgiveness Is Available

A guy received his paycheck and the amount was $100 too much. The next week they corrected it and took out $100. So the man went to the payroll office and complained about their making errors. They said, "Well, you didn't complain last week."

The man said, "Yeah, I can tolerate one mistake, but it's getting to be a habit!" We all do sin, regularly, and the dilemma arises when we realize that heaven is a perfect place, so how can the imperfect get there? The answer — only through Jesus Christ can we be cleansed.

One of the best motivations for wanting people to become Christians is the forgiveness that is available to those who place their trust in Christ. The promise of forgiveness not only provides you with a solid hope, it also gives you a solid reason to want to share your faith.

If ever there was a time when society needed some promises to stand on, now is the time. Every Christian needs to be reminded on a regular basis of the promise of forgiveness, because we all sin. The apostle Paul said, "There is no one righteous" (Romans 3:10), and "all have sinned and fall short of the glory of God" (Romans 3:23). We all make mistakes.

Here are some promises about forgiveness that the Christian can hold on to.

Forgiveness Is a Fact — Believe It

"Therefore, there is now no condemnation for those who are in Christ Jesus, because through Christ Jesus the law of the Spirit of life set me free from the law of sin and death" (Romans 8:1-2).

Whenever you see the word "therefore," you have to go back to the previous passage and see what it's "there" "for." You need to realize that back in Romans 7, Paul has just given the church at Rome a very transparent look into his own personal struggles. And he admits to occasional defeats in his life. Paul says, "I do not understand what I do. For what I want to do I do not do, but what I hate I do" (Romans 7:15).

Later in the chapter Paul says, "What a wretched man I am!" (Romans 7:24). If the apostle Paul is wretched, what am I? (Don't answer that.) But do understand that I can relate to his frustrations.

Paul says, "What a wretched man I am. Who will rescue me from this body of death?" And then he answers his own question, "Thanks be to God — through Jesus Christ our Lord!" (Romans 7:24-25).

Charles Swindoll, in his book, *The Finishing Touch*, writes,

> God's book is a veritable storehouse of promises — over 7,000 of them. Not empty hopes and dreams, not just nice sounding eloquently worded thoughts that make you feel warm all over, but promises. Verbal guarantees in writing, signed by the Creator himself, in which he declares he will do, or refrain from doing specific things.
>
> In a world of liars, cheats, deceivers and con artists, isn't it a relief to know that there is someone you can trust? If he said it, you can count on it.*

---

*Charles Swindoll, *The Finishing Touch* (Dallas: Word, 1994), p. 78.

In our world we're not used to such honesty. The apostle Paul is assuring his readers that forgiveness is promised for those who are in Christ. Forgiveness is a fact — believe it. But I think there are three reasons why we find forgiveness difficult to believe. One reason is that . . .

Some Have the Wrong Image of God

How do you view God? It will determine whether you believe He can and will forgive you. You may have grown up with a picture of God as your least favorite teacher, or a bully of a policeman who was always looking over your shoulder, waiting to blow the whistle when you mess up.

But that type of picture doesn't even come close to the biblical picture of God. Not too long ago I had a flight from Albuquerque to St. Louis, and it was rather obvious that it had been badly overbooked. When I checked in, I mentioned that I would volunteer to take a later flight. (For those of you who travel a lot, you know that, translated, that means, "Give me a free ticket and I'll get home a couple of hours later than I planned.")

The couple seated next to me in the terminal were pretty upset because it looked like only one of them would be able to get a seat on the flight. So while they were pleading their case I reiterated to the ticket agent that I was willing to take another flight.

The woman next to me overheard my conversation and was overcome with appreciation. She said to me, "You are so gracious." And then she told her husband and about twenty other passengers, "This man has volunteered to take a later flight, so that we can fly together. You are so gracious!"

And I just said, "Well, no problem. Hope it works out for you guys." For the next few minutes I sat there feeling kind of philanthropic, and also a little guilty that I hadn't revealed my ulterior motives. About that time over the loudspeaker the ticket agent said, "Ladies and gentlemen, as you can see our flight is full today."

He then pointed at me and said, "One person has already volunteered to take a later flight in exchange for a free round trip flight anywhere in the continental United States. Please let me know if anyone else wants to take advantage of this great opportunity."

When he said that, I could feel my face starting to turn red with embarrassment. Even the couple next to me looked at me and smirked. I said, "I'm not nearly as gracious as you thought I was, am I?" Fortunately, they kind of chuckled.

Christ is so different from me and anyone else for that matter. His forgiveness has no strings attached, no ulterior motives, no hidden agenda. It's not for his benefit, it's for ours.

But that is why Christ came to earth as God in the flesh — to teach us about the nature of God. Wander the streets of Palestine in the first century and watch what Jesus does. To a paralyzed man in Mark 2, Jesus says, "Your sins are forgiven" (Mark 2:5). To an adulterous woman in John 8 he says, "Neither do I condemn you. Go now and leave your life of sin" (John 8:11). Or while the perfect lamb of God is dying on a cross and being taunted by the crowd, He says, "Father, forgive them, for they do not know what they are doing" (Luke 23:34). I see that scene and I am encouraged. For if he can forgive them, then he can forgive me.

The Bible says, "But if we walk in the light, as he is in the light, we have fellowship with one another, and the blood of Jesus, his Son, purifies us from all sin" (1 John 1:7).

Another reason people have a difficult time believing that forgiveness is a fact is that . . .

Justice Is Logical, Grace Is Illogical

It just doesn't make sense. Back in the 1880s in Newark, Ohio, there was a man named Neal Johnston. Johnston was known to others as a good man with a bad temper. One day he got into an argument with his neighbor over a property line. That line dispute between the two got so out of hand that it turned into a fight — a fight in which Johnston killed his neighbor.

He was sentenced to life imprisonment at the Ohio State Penitentiary. That was back in the days when life actually meant life. Each month his family would make the journey from Newark to Columbus to visit him. Over the years Johnston had shown true remorse for his actions and had gained the respect of the inmates, along with those who worked at the prison.

Back then it was the custom of the state of Ohio that each Christmas the governor would release one prisoner upon the recommendation of the warden. Of course, those who were in for life were never seriously considered. But on the Christmas morning nearly twelve years from the time of the murder all of the inmates quietly filed into the room in silence anticipating the announcement of who would be freed.

The warden said the name, "Neal Johnston." There was no response. Again the warden said, "Neal Johnston, would you come to the front?" But no one stepped forward. The warden began walking through the rows searching for Johnston until he found a man on his knees leaning against the wall sobbing. It was Neal Johnston. He kept saying one phrase over and over, "There must be some mistake! There must be some mistake!"

The warden put his hand on his shoulder and said, "There is no mistake, Neal. The pardon is real."

When I look at myself and see my sin, and when I look at Calvary and see forgiveness, in disbelief I say, "There must be some mistake!"

But then my gentle Shepherd puts His hand on my shoulder and says, "There is no mistake, Dave. The pardon is real."

That's the message that the unsaved need to hear — not some holier than thou, "straighten up your life or else" verbal thrashing. If you want people to see a sermon through your life, then admit your weaknesses to them, inform them that you have turned these areas over to the Lord, and stress the fact that God has forgiven you and He would love to do the same for them. Wayne Smith often reminds people that the church is a hospital for sinners, not a sanctuary for saints. And I believe that more people can be reached for Christ when they realize God's unconditional love for each of us through the promise of forgiveness.

Another reason forgiveness is difficult to believe is . . .

You Don't Feel Forgiven

Satan keeps you feeling that way by casting doubt. It's like the couple who was having marriage problems, so they decided to go to a counselor. The man said, "Doctor, everytime we get in an argument, she gets historical!"

The counselor said, "Uh, you mean hysterical."

The man said, "No, I mean historical. She always brings up my past."

Does Satan ever get historical with you? He does with me. He specializes in haunting us with the memory of our mistakes. Satan is a video genius when it comes to splicing together a highlight film of your burdensome blunders and then showing them to you. Warren Wiersbe says, "We must learn from the past, not live in the past."

And so sometimes you might not feel forgiven, but remember forgiveness is not contingent on feeling, it's based on fact, the truth of the Scriptures.

Maybe it's time for you to stop allowing Satan to hold

you hostage with his reminders of your past...that display of uncontrolled anger, the time you got drunk and embarassed your loved ones, that cutting remark you've regretted for years, or that one night stand. If you are a Christian, and you have sincerely repented before God, then it's time to trust Him for the forgiveness He's promised you through the blood of Jesus Christ. So the next time Satan reminds you of your past, you remind him of his future!

Forgiveness Is a Gift — Accept It

"For what the law was powerless to do in that it was weakened by the sinful nature, God did by sending his own Son in the likeness of sinful man to be a sin offering. And so he condemned sin in sinful man, in order that the righteous requirements of the law might be fully met in us, who do not live according to the sinful nature but according to the Spirit" (Romans 8:3-4).

Through His atoning death Jesus has given you the gift of forgiveness and salvation. It is only available to you if you accept it. You could bring me a huge birthday present, and say, "Here's a gift for you." But if I reject it, or if I never open it, then the gift is meaningless. For the gift to serve a purpose it must be accepted; that's why the Bible speaks of receiving Christ (John 1:12).

Just as heaven gives the Christian hope for the future, forgiveness gives the Christian hope for today. There are so many people whom you can influence for the Lord by introducing them to the One who can erase their past and at the same time empower their present.

Freedom is not a license to do what is wrong; it is the liberty to do what is right. In Romans 6:1-2 Paul says, "What shall we say, then? Shall we go on sinning so that grace many increase? By no means! We died to sin; how can we live in it any longer?"

We've got to accept the free gift of forgiveness. Since we can't understand or explain why God would forgive and forget our sins we don't always accept that forgiveness. And the guilt continues to eat away.

Amazing Grace

Not too long ago I received a card from one of my church members. She wrote,

> Although God forgives me of my sin, I have not been able to forgive myself of one, and now that I know what stands in the way of faith, maybe I'll be able to forgive MYSELF, so I don't place blame on God.

> About ten years ago I was in an abusive relationship and although I have always been pro-life, when I became pregnant I chose to not only abort my child, but I also aborted my beliefs and trust in God. It cuts like a knife when I hear someone mention abortion. It never goes away.

Let me assure you, that is a letter that Planned Parenthood won't publish in their newsletter. That letter represents ten years of pain and guilt. I share that because it is representative of many who will be reading this book. For you maybe it wasn't an abortion, but it was something else. Whatever the skeleton in your closet, it continues to hold you hostage. It is difficult to share with a non-believer the relief which comes from God's "amazing grace" if you truly haven't accepted it yourself.

Please remember, Christ died on a cross because of every sin you and I will ever commit.

Second Corinthians 7:10 says, "Godly sorrow brings repentance that leads to salvation and leaves no regret, but worldly sorrow brings death." You see, there is a good kind of guilt. The Bible calls it godly sorrow. It leads to repentance and genuine change. There is also bad guilt, worldly sorrow, the type which plagues and enslaves.

In Richard Hoefler's book, *Will Daylight Come?* he includes a story of the freedom which forgiveness can give.

A little boy visiting his grandparents was given his first slingshot. He practiced in the woods, but he could never hit his target.

As he came back to Grandma's backyard, he spied her pet duck. On an impulse he took aim and let it fly. The stone hit, and the duck fell dead. The boy panicked. Desperately he hid the dead duck in the woodpile, only to look up and see his sister watching. Sally had seen it all, but she said nothing.

After lunch that day, Grandma said, "Sally, let's wash the dishes."

But Sally said, "Johnny told me he wanted to help in the kitchen today, didn't you, Johnny? " And she whispered to him, "Remember the duck!" So Johnny did the dishes.

Later Grandpa asked if the children wanted to go fishing. Grandma said, "I'm sorry, but I need Sally to help make supper." Sally smiled and said, "That's all taken care of. Johnny wants to do it." Again she whispered, "Remember the duck." Johnny stayed while Sally went fishing.

After several days of Johnny doing both his chores and Sally's, he couldn't stand it. He confessed to Grandma that he'd killed the duck.

"I know, Johnny," she said, giving him a hug, "I was standing at the window and saw the whole thing. Because I love you, I forgave. I just wondered how long you would let Sally make a slave of you."*

The message of forgiveness is a sermon you can live — not just preach. One of the greatest testimonies that the saved can show to the lost is that you have accepted God's forgiveness. If Jesus were here in the flesh and He saw the anguish that you continue to allow Satan to put you

---

*Richard Hoefler, *Will Daylight Come?* (Lima, OH: CSS Publishing Co., 1979), n.p.

through over past sins of which you have already repented, I think He'd say, "I suffered enough on the cross; there's no reason to allow your past to paralyze your power in the present."

The psalmist said, "As far as the east is from the west, he has removed our transgressions from us" (Psalm 103:12). Do you believe it? Don't torture yourself by thinking, "He can forgive everybody else's sin, but not mine. I'm different."

How arrogant! He forgave Saul, a murderer of Christians. He forgave David, an adulterer. He forgave Zacchaeus, a liar and a cheat. The list goes on and on, from the respected to the promiscuous. But He can't forgive you? Hmm.

The Bible says, "If we confess our sins, he is faithful and just and will forgive us our sins and purify us from all unrighteousness" (1 John 1:9). Forgiveness is a fact to be believed and a gift to be received.

A Father's Love

I remember an October morning, at three a.m., when my daughter Savannah, who was six at the time, awakened me. From her room she said, "Daddy, Daddy, I'm worried."

In a semi-comatose voice I said, "What is it?"

She replied, "I left my turtle out in the backyard."

Being the sensitive father I am I said, "So?"

She continued her passionate request by saying, "I'm afraid he'll climb out of his box and I'll never see him again."

I tersely said, "Honey, I'm sleeping now, I'll do it the first thing in the morning."

Her pleading went on, "Please, Daddy."

Beth rolled over and said, "Oh, go on Dave, just go do it real quickly."

And I thought, you go do it! (I thought that. I didn't say that!) I said, "I am not going outside at three in the morning to bring some turtle inside. You'll see — she'll fall back asleep in a minute."

There was silence for about ten seconds, and I kind of smiled. Then from the other room I heard this little voice say, "Please, Daddy."

Well, for some reason I immediately sprang out of bed to go and rescue the turtle. Before I left the room I looked at my wife and said, "What am I doing?"

And I'll never forget what she said. Beth said, "You're being a father."

So I shuffled out the door, into the backyard (in my underwear). I located the box, and fortunately the turtle was still there. (I might add, he was sound asleep and enjoying it.)

I brought him inside and told Savannah the good news. And then I went back to bed, amazingly content that my daughter felt comfortable in asking me to do a favor for her, and thankful that she trusted that I would come through for her.

If I, as an imperfect father, am willing to do the illogical because of love, what about a perfect heavenly Father? God's love is so unconditional for His children that He is willing to forgive those who place their trust in Him. And Satan scratches his head and says, "But look at their sins! How can you forgive them? What are you doing?

And God smiles and answers, "I'm being a father." Oh, not begrudgingly or out of obligation but because He wants to; not out of duty but out of devotion.

Jesus said, "Which of you, if his son asks for bread, will give him a stone? Or if he asks for a fish, will give him a snake? If you, then, though you are evil, know how to give good gifts to your children, how much more will your Father in heaven give good gifts to those who ask him!" (Matthew 7:9-11).

115

The Bottom Line

Several years ago, Adolph Coors IV shared his Christian testimony in a service at the church where I serve. I'll never forget his conclusion. He said, "If man's greatest need would have been for pleasure, then God would have sent an entertainer. If man's greatest need would have been for money, then He would have sent a financial consultant. If man's greatest need would have been information, He would have sent an educator.

"But God in His infinite wisdom knew that man's greatest need was forgiveness, and so He sent a Savior."

Paul said, "Therefore, there is now no condemnation for those who are in Christ Jesus" (Romans 8:1).

Hell Is Terrible

It was the teenager's first job. He was a delivery boy for a florist. One day the boy had the responsibility of delivering two sets of flowers. One was for a funeral home and the other was for a big church that had relocated to a larger sanctuary.

The florist knew there was a problem when he received a phone call from an irate minister. The preacher said, "We've got a beautiful new sanctuary with a set of flowers up front which say, 'Rest in Peace.'"

The florist said, "You think you've got problems. Somewhere in this city there is a set of flowers beside a casket with a sign which says, 'Good Luck in your New Location!'"

When it comes to your final destination, luck will play no role in determining where you spend eternity. Choice, not chance, will determine your direction. The Bible teaches that beyond the grave you will be assigned to either eternal life in heaven or eternal death in hell. "Just as man is destined to die once, and after that to face judgment" (Hebrews 9:27).

A number of years ago I spoke with a lady in Lexington, Kentucky who claimed to be an atheist. She didn't believe in God, or heaven and hell. Toward the end of our conversation I said, "Let's say I'm wrong — according to you I will have lost nothing and I will gain nothing. But if you are wrong you have everything to lose and nothing to gain."

And she looked at me and said, "That's a risk I'm willing to take."

We live in a culture in which we are surrounded by multitudes who seem to be content to "roll the dice" on their spiritual destiny.

This chapter will focus upon the frightening reality of hell. May it remind you of why you want to avoid going there. I also hope that it will inspire you to lovingly and aggressively share your faith so that those within your sphere of influence will experience the eternal joy of heaven rather than the punishment of hell.

Hell Is a Literal Place

C.S. Lewis said, "There is no doctrine which I would more willingly remove from Christianity than this, if it lay in my power. But it has the full support of Scripture and, specially, of our Lord's own words."*

If God in His word states even one time that there is a place called hell then those who believe the Bible must accept it as the truth. But the Bible doesn't talk about it just once, it talks about it fifty-four times.

Do you know who talked about hell more than anyone else? Your gentle shepherd, Jesus Christ. He believed in hell.

I believe hell is a literal place not only because of what the Bible says and because of what Jesus taught but also because justice demands it.

In 1912 J. Henry Jowett addressed the Yale Convention. Jowett said, "The very term 'good news' implies that

---

*C.S. Lewis, *The Problem of Pain* (London: Geoffrey Bles, 1940), p. 106.

there is such a thing as bad news, the very proclamation of salvation presupposes a state of being lost. Hell is the dark background on which the brilliant picture of the gospel is painted. But without the background you have no picture."

Any justice system is governed by a punishment for those who break the rules. People say, "Don't worry. What goes around comes around; he'll get his. Someday it will catch up with him." That's justice. A few years ago several cars were broken into in my neighborhood. One morning I came out to my car and there was a gaping hole in my dashboard where previously my stereo had resided.

I just sat there and couldn't stop laughing, because for the past year that crazy stereo hadn't worked. It had become a constant source of frustration to me. I could just picture this thief giving a great sales pitch only to have the prospective buyer try it out and find it doesn't work. That's justice!

I called my insurance company, and even though my stereo had been on the blink, they said that they would still reimburse me for the cost of the stereo. Now that's miraculous!

The justice system was in progress, and if the thief ever gets caught, he'll have to face the music. (No pun intended.) But the truth of the matter is not every thief gets caught, not every stolen stereo is broken, and not every insurance company would pay that claim.

Simple logic demands that there be some type of judgment. Even unbelievers reach the same conclusion as the believers that there must be rewards for those who obey and punishment for those who don't.

If there is no hell, then Calvary was a tragic mistake. For if there is no pending punishment, then there is no need for a pardon.

Hell Is Intense Pain

A number of years ago the infamous atheist Madalyn Murray O'Hair spoke on the campus of Drake University. She blasted the Bible and Christ and the reality of heaven and hell. She said, "Who wants to go to a place where all they do is sing hymns and play harps? Speaking for myself, I'd rather go to hell!"

Well, she must be speaking for herself. She sure isn't speaking for me. I don't want to go to hell. "There is a way that seems right to man, but in the end it leads to death" (Proverbs 14:12). The Bible assures us that it is a place of intense pain.

Emotional Suffering

The New Testament uses two words when speaking of hell. One is Hades, which generally means the place of the dead. The other is Gehenna, which is the place of retribution for evil deeds. The term "Gehenna" doesn't mean much to us in today's setting. But to the Jew who would hear Jesus describe this place of punishment as Gehenna, it communicated volumes.

Outside of Jerusalem was a garbage dump which burned and smoldered constantly. The people of the city would take their trash and toss it over a wall, and it would roll down into this deep ravine which was always on fire. It was called Gehenna.

The mention of the term must have conjured up feelings of worthlessness and pain. Bill Hybels says, "The person who wakes up and finds himself in Gehenna must realize that the God of the universe who gave him so much value in life has trashed him for eternity."

Perhaps it is the same feeling of worthlessness that Christ experienced on the cross when God the Father painfully looked the other way. No wonder Jesus said, "My God, my God, why have you forsaken me?" (Matthew 27:46).

Physical Suffering

Listen to some of his descriptions of this terrible place: a place of torments and everlasting punishment, a place where people pray and scream for mercy and weep and wail, a furnace of fire, a place of torments, a place of outer darkness, and a place where the worm never dies and the fire is not quenched. The physical pain in hell will be excruciating.

Maybe you heard about the wealthy landowner who was seated on the front porch when two guys came walking past. He said, "Would you like to make some money by chopping wood for me? I'll pay you each $15 an hour."

Neither of them had ever chopped wood in their lives. But since they were both in college, suffering from the disease of mal-tuition, they figured for $15 an hour they could learn.

After the man got them started in his back yard, his telephone rang. It was his buddy from work with the untimely news that their entertainment for the big company party that night had just cancelled. The caller inquired, "Where can we find quality entertainment on such short notice?"

The wealthy man answered, "I don't know." But about that time he looked out his back kitchen window and one of the guys who had been chopping wood went running across the backyard, did a triple cartwheel, raced up the side of the garage, did a double backflip, and landed perfectly on his feet.

The man walked out into his backyard and excitedly asked the other guy, "Do you think that your buddy would do that at my party at work tonight for $100?"

His friend said, "I don't know, let me ask him. Hey Fred, are you willing to chop off another toe for $100?"

As strange as it might seem, Jesus spoke of a circumstance when you might need to do the same thing. Oh not

121

for some extra money, but as a safeguard from landing in hell for eternity.

Jesus said, "If your right hand causes you to sin, cut it off and throw it away. It is better for you to lose one part of your body than for your whole body to go into hell" (Matthew 5:30).

In today's culture the application would be, if your job, a close relationship, a car, or a cabin on the lake interferes with your Christian life then get rid of it. It's better to remove those things and inherit eternal life than to be so wrapped up in the things of this world that you end up in hell.

It was the theologian Zwingli who said, "If you possess something that you are not able to part with, then you don't possess it, it possesses you." It's true you can't take it with you. (Even if you could, it would probably melt!)

Over five times in the Gospel of Matthew, hell is described as a place of "weeping and gnashing of teeth."

Relational Suffering

Mark Twain said, "I'll take heaven for the climate, but hell for the company." Some people share this false impression that in hell all the "bad" people get to hang out together. They picture a perpetual Mardi Gras Party! Not quite. Part of what makes hell, hell, is the lack of fellowship. Hell can be described as a place of separation — solitary suffering forever.

When I was about six years old, my father and I were in a Kroger's store together. We got separated, so I frantically started looking down each aisle trying to find him. After a couple of minutes I began to panic. But just about that time I heard a horrendously loud sneeze in the aisle next to me.

When my dad sneezed, you knew it was my dad. He was easy to find then — I just followed the sound of falling cereal boxes. Now that was a terrifying experience for a little kid, (being lost — not the sneeze). But I was only separated momentarily from my dad. Can you imagine what it is like to be eternally separated from your heavenly Father, the One who created you?

Bill Hybels says, "In hell, God chooses to be conspicuous by His absence."

Eternal Suffering

Jesus said, "They will go away to eternal punishment, but the righteous to eternal life" (Matthew 25:46).

If you are a music lover, you may recall the rock group "Wham." George Michael was the lead singer before he embarked on a solo career. They had a song out entitled, "Freedom." It spoke of how great a love a guy had for his girl and how he would do anything to prove his love for her.

In one section the lyrics say, "You could take me to hell, and back, just as long as we're together." Many in our culture have bought into that philosophy. But the Bible tells us it's not true. You see, there is no gal or guy worth going to hell for, because once you go there, you can't come back. It's eternal.

The apostle Paul said, "They will be punished with everlasting destruction and shut out from the presence of God" (2 Thessalonians 1:9). The welcome sign to hell should read, "The Point of No Return." There is no end and there is no exit in hell. It is a literal place.

Hell Is a Personal Choice

Years ago there was a car repair commercial which had a mechanic saying, "You can pay me now, or you can pay me later." There is no escaping the Judgment. At some point every knee will bow. You can bow now, or you can bow when it's too late. Jesus said, "Whoever believes and is baptized will be saved, but whoever does not believe will be condemned" (Mark 16:16). In other words, hell is a personal choice.

Years ago an evangelist told a story which really showed me the lengths to which God went to keep me from a place called hell.

Back in the old west there was a young man who had been raised with Christian principles, but as he got older, he departed from his upbringing. He decided to branch out and open up a saloon. So he advertised the grand opening, but when the appointed time came, no one showed up. After some time of frustration, he looked out the window and was surprised to see that his father was out in front. His dad was talking people out of entering the saloon.

The young man went outside, and yelled, "Dad, you're ruining my grand opening."

His father replied, "Son, I can't let anyone go in there. Alcohol will ruin their lives, steal their money, and destroy their family."

About that time another man came up and the father proceeded to dissuade him from entering. The son was so furious, that he pulled his fist back and punched his father in the face and knocked him to the ground.

The father looked up at his boy and said, "Son, you can hit me, you can spit on me, you can even kill me. But the only way anyone is going in there is over my dead body."

People ask me, "Would a loving God send someone to hell?" The answer is no. You send yourself. At different junctions in life you are introduced to Christ. And you are given the opportunity to realize that He died on a cross in order that you could be saved from your sins. And Jesus hangs on a cross which stands right before the entrance to hell. He looks at you and says, "The only way you'll ever go in there is over my dead body."

The Bottom Line

Former Lexington, Kentucky, preacher Wayne Smith has said, "Satan won't tell you there's no hell, and he won't tell you there's no heaven, but he will tell you there's no hurry."

Eternity hangs in the balance. The world needs to be lovingly led to the foot of the cross. As terrible as hell is, the person who swallows his pride and places his trust in Christ, need not worry for he will never have to see the place. While fear shouldn't be the only motivation for accepting Christ, it is a valid motivation. The wisest man in the Old Testament said, "The fear of the Lord is the beginning of wisdom" (Proverbs 9:10).

Throughout life you are given opportunities where someone brings you face to face with what Christ did for you. You can accept his gracious gift of eternal life or reject it. It's your decision.

Heaven Is Incredible

Occasionally I'll read the story of *Alice in Wonderland* to my children. There is a place in the story where Alice pops out of a hole and she comes to a fork in the road. The Cheshire Cat is sitting right there. Alice looks down one direction and then the other way and asks the Cat, "Would you tell me, please, which way I ought to go from here?"

"That depends a good deal on where you want to get to," said the Cat.

"I don't much care where —" said Alice.

"Then it doesn't matter which way you go," said the Cat.*

We live among a people who don't know where they're going. In fact, many don't even care. Jesus said, "For wide is the gate and broad is the road that leads to destruction, and many enter through it. But small is the gate and narrow the road that leads to life, and only a few find it" (Matthew 7:13-14).

Many are so preoccupied with the here and now, so locked in the present, they haven't bothered to give the future much thought. You may recall a number of years

---

*Lewis Carroll, *Alice in Wonderland* (New York: Clarkson N. Potter, 1973), p. 55.

ago when a movie came out entitled, *Heaven Can Wait*. John Turner, preacher at Mason Church of Christ, Mason, OH, told me, "Nothing is more blatant than to have a culture's philosophy summarized on a marquee."

Times certainly have changed. How different from the previous generation which sang, "Oh, Lord, I want to be in that number, when the saints go marchin' in." But you can make a difference. Through your manner and message you can point the hellbound toward heaven.

There are plenty of reasons that I am excited about heaven, but in this chapter I'll focus on three areas.

The Beauty of a New Community

This earth was created to continually remind us of God's awesome power. Genesis tells us that this universe was created in six days. Maybe you've gone to the Grand Canyon or to either the Atlantic or Pacific Ocean. Perhaps you've been to the mountains of Colorado or the islands of Hawaii. Those are beautiful places, but none compare with the beauty of the new community in heaven.

A few years ago there was a great songwriter named Keith Green. He talked of God's creating this beautiful earth in six days. But he posed the question, "Can you imagine what Heaven will be like? He's been working on Heaven for 2,000 years!" We cannot fathom that.

Jesus said, "In my Father's house are many rooms; if it were not so, I would have told you. I am going there to prepare a place for you. And if I go and prepare a place for you, I will come back and take you to be with me that you also may be where I am (John 14:2-3).

The apostle John describes his vision of heaven coming down to the new earth by saying, "It shone with the glory of God, and its brilliance was like that of a very precious jewel" (Revelation 21:11).

It had the glory of God upon it. Do you remember those

lines you had in the Christmas pageant when you were just a kid? On the night Jesus was born, there were shepherds keeping watch over their flocks by night in the fields by Bethlehem, and, lo, the glory of the Lord shone round about them.

That same glory which shone upon the fields of Bethlehem shines on the new Jerusalem and the new earth. People there need no light from the sun nor the moon; it must be radiantly beautiful!

The songwriter said, "When we've been there ten thousand years, bright shining as the sun, we've no less days to sing God's praise than when we first begun." The Christian will be able to enjoy the beauty of a new community for eternity.

The Blessings of a New Companionship

In heaven you will be able to see Jesus face to face, to fall at His feet and worship Him. You can walk with Him and talk with Him. He'll enjoy clearing up all the mysteries and questions which have confused you. He'll answer all your "Whys?" This new companionship will allow you to go ever deeper in your journey with Jesus.

Nowadays, many people have bought into the popular but false notion that we are all headed for heaven. But if you don't have a companionship with Christ prior to eternity, you can't expect a new relationship with Him in eternity.

You may recall that the reason many Bible characters got persecuted wasn't because they believed in Jehovah God. They were persecuted because they claimed He was the *only* God. Rulers and religious leaders couldn't stomach that. They thought, "How exclusive! How intolerant to say that He is the only way."

Sound familiar? Ever had anyone challenge your beliefs with the convenient fall-back position of "all roads lead to heaven"? Don't get me wrong, it's a great concept; it's very reassuring. There's only one problem with it. It is in direct opposition to the teachings of the One whom death could not keep. For Jesus said, "I am the way and the truth and the life. No one comes to the Father except through me" (John 14:6).

So the theory of "believe what you want, we're all heading to the same place," may be a true statement — if heaven is not the place that you're talking about! While it may be convenient, comforting, and a way to avoid conflict, it is not the truth. Love compels you to tell people how they can get to heaven.

Just as marriage is different from dating, in heaven your relationship with Christ will be new and fresh. God's Word confirms that by comparing it to one of the most beautiful sights you can picture. He speaks of a bride on her wedding day. Now my wife looks great all the time — but on the day we got married, she was even more beautiful!

There are two reasons this is true: preparation and anticipation. When a woman gets married she spends hours preparing her hair and her face and her dress. She wants to look her best. I conduct about twenty weddings a year, and I have never seen an ugly bride.

Preparation

What type of bride would rush into the church ten minutes before the wedding, toss on a dress, comb her hair with her fingers, and say, "I don't need to brush my teeth, I already did this week!"

No, that's not what happens. There are months of dating and talking. There are weeks of planning for the ceremony, reception and honeymoon. On the day of the wedding, hours are spent improving appearance. Manicures are scheduled, banquet rooms reserved, hair stylists hired. Why all the fuss? Because something is about to change. It's no longer a dating relationship, now it's marriage. It is a new companionship.

Anticipation

But it's not just the preparation, it's also the anticipation. The organ strikes a chord and everyone stands. (The mother of the bride starts to cry as she recalls that girls tend to marry guys who remind them of their father!) This is the moment they've been waiting for. They have literally been counting down the days and the hours.

And as the bride moves down closer to the groom she sees that he is grinning from ear to ear. And he whispers, "You are beautiful; I've waited a long time for this moment." She is the picture of purity because she has prepared and waited for this day.

John says, "I saw the holy city, the new Jerusalem, coming down out of heaven from God, prepared as a bride beautifully dressed for her husband" (Revelation 21:2).

We all have relationships which are special. They challenge us, strengthen us, encourage us and sustain us. You learn pretty quickly that while the undertaker may be the last one to let you down, there are still plenty of others who disappoint. Your best friend may unknowingly hurt you. Your spouse may discourage you. But in heaven, you can say good-bye to divorce, backstabbing, income-tax returns, severed relationships, allergies, pink slips, pulled muscles, cancer and Kaopectate. They are not allowed inside. The companionship that will supersede all others will be the one with Jesus Christ.

John describes the new companionship by saying, "Now the dwelling of God is with men, and he will live with them. They will be his people, and God himself will be with them and be their God" (Revelation 21:3).

Dr. Nelson Bell said, "Only those who are prepared to

die are really prepared to live."

Just Inside the Gate

Before going to work for Walt Disney, Derek Johnson traveled the country with a contemporary Christian singing group called "Regeneration." Sometimes through the course of a concert Johnson would tell the story of his little five-year-old daughter getting lost while shopping with her mother. She was just one aisle over but she was petrified.

Johnson would go on and explain to the audience that for a long time she was afraid of crowds and would cling to her parents. During that period they had a family devotion about heaven. When it was over she asked, "Daddy, will there be a lot of people in heaven?"

Johnson answered, "Yes, there will be millions."

She nervously said, "How will I find you and mommy in heaven?"

Johnson realized that was her major concern. So he wanted to give her an answer that would satisfy her. So Johnson said, "Tell you what, let's meet just inside the gate."

She asked, "Daddy, is there more than one gate in heaven?"

He remembered reading in Revelation that their are four walls and three gates in each wall, so he said, "Yes, there are twelve gates in heaven."

The persistent daughter continued her interrogation, "Which gate?"

Johnson said he replied, "I'll tell you what; when you get to heaven, you just ask someone which way is east and you walk until you come to the eastern wall. Then find the middle gate. Let's all meet just inside the middle eastern gate."

And with that Johnson said, "I kissed her goodnight,

and said, 'Now remember where we're going to meet.'"

And his daughter interrupted and said, "Just inside the middle eastern gate."

Derek Johnson said, "From that time on seldom would we say goodbye without one of us saying, 'Meet you just inside,' and the other would respond, 'The middle eastern gate'."

In the concert, Johnson would then turn to one of the girls in the group and ask, "Is that story true?"

And she would smile and say, "Yes it is."

Johnson would say, "How do you know?"

And the singer would reply, "Because I was that little girl." And then she would add, "Meet you just inside . . ."

And Derek Johnson would say, "The middle eastern gate."

Wow! Can you begin to fathom what it will be like to be reunited with your loved ones in heaven someday, just inside the gate? To go together as a family and sit at the feet of Jesus. A new relationship with family, friends and your Savior. God promises that heaven will be a perfect place without sorrow or frustration. "He will wipe every tear from their eyes. There will be no more death or mourning or crying or pain, for the old order of things has passed away" (Revelation 21:4).

To be in a perfect relationship with the one who made heaven a reality for those who trusted in Him! Larry Moody, Bible Study leader for the PGA Tour, says, "The Christian must remember that you are not in the land of the living going to the land of the dying. You are in the land of the dying, going to the land of the living."

The Benefits of a New Creation

Ever wish that you could change something about your appearance? Years ago when Jane Fonda traveled across the country promoting her fitness video she said, "I have yet to meet a person who is completely satisfied with their body the way it is." Heaven will provide you with the opportunity for a new creation. When you move into eternity, the apostle Paul assures you that you can have a new, glorified body.

He writes, "But our citizenship is in heaven. And we eagerly await a Savior from there, the Lord Jesus Christ, who, by the power that enables him to bring everything under his control, will transform our lowly bodies so that they will be like his glorious body" (Philippians 3:20-21). For some of us, receiving a new and improved body in itself will be paradise!

The Christian will have a glorified body. Not in six weeks or your money back, but immediately. "In a flash, in the the twinkling of an eye, . . . we will be changed" (1 Corinthians 15:51-52).

Jenni Smith had it all going for her. She was a committed Christian and played the keyboards for a Christian band. She had excelled in gymnastic competitions for years and in two months she would begin her senior year of high school. On a July morning in 1989, Jenni along with the rest of the cheerleaders from the Christian Academy of Louisville were warming up at Seneca Park. Jenni did a back handspring as she had done thousands of times before, but she slipped as she landed on the wet grass. The result? Jenni was paralyzed from the neck down.

After several months in a hospital she was able to return to school with the aid of a motorized wheelchair. With the help of friends and tutors, and through her own courage and determination, she was able to graduate with her classmates. I'll never forget the Commencement services.

When her name was called she rode across the stage and the principal placed her diploma on the tray of her electric wheelchair. All in attendance gave her a standing ovation, and then reached for a tissue to try to stop the flood of tears.

Later during the service I flipped through the program. Since it was a small class, beside each graduate's picture was their favorite Scripture verse. My curiosity drew me to Jenni's picture and verse. It said, "Isaiah 40:30-31." It didn't need to be written out for me to know what it said, and why Jenni loved it. The girl who could no longer walk, run, flip or cartwheel chose this as her favorite. You remember the prophet's words:

"But those who hope in the Lord will renew their strength. They will soar on wings like eagles; they will run and not grow weary, they will walk and not be faint" (Isaiah 40:31). Heaven will take care of Jenni's physical problems in an instant!

That is the benefit of the new creation in heaven. Dante said, "Life without hope is hell." The Christian has hope because of a place called heaven.

As a Christian you have the responsibility to try to remind people of the benefits of heaven. Regardless of the adversity you face or the ridicule you receive in trying to reach the unbeliever, keep showing them the way to heaven.

The Bottom Line

A father walked past his son's bedroom late one evening and saw a ray of light from beneath the door. The dad cracked the door and saw his son reading a wild west novel. The boy kept saying over and over again, "You're gonna get it, you're gonna get it."

His dad stepped into the room and asked, "What are you doing?"

The boy explained, "I was reading this novel and the villain kept getting the best of the hero. So I skipped to the end of the book and read the last chapter. So now whenever the villain is getting the best of the hero I just laugh and say, 'You're gonna get it."

When the present looks bleak, then remember you have hope for the future. There is a big difference between what is temporary and what is eternal. The boy is right. If you know the end of the story, then you're not overly concerned with the development of the plot. Like the boy, I have read the end of the Book, and we win.

Someday, I want to go home — home to heaven. Can you imagine that, standing face to face with Jesus. Max Lucado describes him as the "One who refuses to remember my sins." I look forward to seeing Jesus.

And I want to see my grandmother Gardner, my mother-in-law, and my Dado Stone. I want to see my Uncle Greg walk for the first time. I want to see the apostle Paul and Esther and Noah. And I want to meet you. Don't you want to be in that number, when the saints go marching in?

Jesus Is Coming Again

A telemarketer called a home in an attempt to try and sell a product. He was greeted by a young boy who whispered, "Hello."

The man inquired, "Is your mom home?"

The boy whispered, "Yes, but she's busy."

The telemarketer tried to go another route by asking, "Well then, is your dad home?"

Again the boy whispered, "Yes, but he's busy."

The perplexed caller said, "Well, are there any other adults in the home?"

The boy whispered, "Yes, the police."

The man said, "Well, can I speak with them?"

The boy whispered, "No, they're busy too."

By this time the caller was beside himself with curiosity. He said, "What are they all doing?"

The boy whispered, "They're looking for me!"

In recent years whenever Jesus has looked down at us from Heaven, He could say the same thing, "They are looking for me, they are waiting for my return." A while back, *U.S. News and World Report* devoted their cover story (December 19, 1994) to the topic of waiting for the Messiah.

I was surprised to read that 61% of Americans believe that Jesus Christ will return to earth. In recent years there has been an increased interest in the Second Coming, partly due to the coming new millennium.

All of the books from Genesis through Malachi could be summed up: Jesus is coming. The books of Matthew through John tell us: Jesus is here. The remaining books from Acts through Revelation are saying: Jesus is coming again. While we may not be certain of exactly when Christ will return, the Scriptures do teach us some basic facts which underscore the importance of being ready for Christ's return.

This chapter is not about different millennial views. Satan enjoys trying to divide the church over secondary issues. Our focus as Christians is upon the fact of Christ's resurrection and His promised return.

Chuck Lee is the Adult Education Minister at the church where I serve. Once he told me why, instead of arguing over the unknown, we should focus upon the resurrection. Chuck said, "A people brought together by a fact of the past, in order to be in fellowship in the present, should not divide themselves over a question of the future."

I believe that God in His wisdom has kept those specifics somewhat veiled so as to heighten the interest and to deepen our study of His word. Tony Campolo says about the Second Coming, "I'm not on the planning committee, I'm on the welcoming committee."

Christians Must Be Encouraged

The Second Coming of Christ has been the ultimate hope of the church since back in the first century. The realization that Jesus will return encourages all of us to look forward to it with great anticipation.

We must have an urgency when it comes to winning the lost. Paul reminds us to "make the most of every opportunity" (Colossians 4:5).

In his first epistle to the Thessalonians, Paul said, "the

coming of the Lord will be like a thief in the night" (1 Thessalonians 5:2). However, he was quick to assure the Christians that Jesus' return should not surprise them like a thief.

His primary purpose in saying that was to suggest that if we're alert, our expectancy will keep us from being caught off guard by His arrival.

You see, when Christ returns for the Christian, it won't be terrifying like the appearance of a thief. It will be an exciting experience, like the anticipated arrival of a long awaited friend.

The Bible says, "We who are still alive and are left will be caught up with them in the clouds to meet the Lord in the air" (1 Thessalonians 4:17). Does that excite you? If you are a Christian it should thrill you. While the fact that Jesus is coming again will be cause for alarm for many in the world, for those who are in Christ, it is a great source of encouragement.

Non-Believers Must Be Warned

Jesus said, "Therefore keep watch because you do not know when the owner of the house will come back — whether in the evening, or at midnight, or when the rooster crows, or at dawn" (Mark 13:35).

It is a Biblical principle that you reap what you sow (Galatians 6:7). Paul Harvey tells of an attractive flight attendant who was annoyed at the flirtatious advances she was receiving from a couple of passengers. One was seated in the front of the plane and one in the back. Throughout the flight she continued to give each of them the cold shoulder and yet each persisted.

As they began their final approach into Chicago, the man up front handed the flight attendant his apartment key along with his address. The flight attendant looked into his eyes, smiled, and then turned and walked toward the back of the plane. She promptly located the other man in the back of the plane, handed him the key and address and whispered, "See you tonight!"

You reap what you sow! What goes around comes around. That is a fact of life. The truth must always come out in the end. When Christ returns, the truth will be evident. There is a payday. There is a time of eternal accounting for the lives we have lived.

"God is just: He will pay back trouble to those who trouble you and give relief to you who are troubled, and to us as well. This will happen when the Lord Jesus is revealed from heaven in blazing fire with his powerful angels" (2 Thessalonians 1:6,7).

Some will be encouraged on that day of Christ's return, but the unbeliever will be discouraged. In fact he will be downright terrified. For in that split second when Christ returns in the sky, he will realize it's too late. He will have to reap what he has sown.

Many people seem to be willing to play Russian roulette with their future. Years ago I recall seeing a sign on an old fenced-in building in downtown Cincinnati. It read: "Warning! Attack dogs on the premises 3 out of 5 nights. You guess which nights." God allows you the free will to make your own choices, but as a Christian who knows the Bible, you have a responsibility to warn the non-believer.

Everyone Must Be Ready

Many of you will recall in September of 1988 a gentleman named Edgar Whisenant was convinced that he had calculated when Christ was going to return. He even printed a booklet called "88 Reasons the Rapture Will Occur in '88." Many disillusioned followers had sold their belongings because of his prediction that Jesus would return on September 10, 11 or 12. At that time I was working at Cincinnati Bible College. To say that the student body had gotten a kick out of the prediction was putting it mildly. When I pulled onto the campus on September 13, as I headed from my car to my office I passed a group of students and jokingly said, "Can you believe it, Edgar was wrong, Jesus didn't return."

And they replied, "You didn't listen to the news this morning, did you?"

I said, "No, what did I miss?

They answered, "Whisenant held a press conference and said that his calculations were a little off. Jesus is going to return today between 10 and 11 a.m. Eastern Standard time."

One of the other guys chimed in and said, "At breakfast, the whole school was buzzing about it."

"Really," I said. At that moment I was faced with a choice. I could go to my office and do some work, or I could have some fun with this. Guess which I chose? Immediately I contacted the head of the maintenance department and asked him to bring me a long rope complete with a pulley. Next I contacted two students who played the trumpet and asked them to meet me in my office. Then I spoke with Mike Shannon, the professor with the largest class which meets on the second floor between 10 and 11 a.m.

My request was simple, keep your side window open and, when you take the roll at the beginning of class, mention the rapture so that people can have that in the back of their minds.

At 10:15, I stood outside the two-and-a-half-story President's Hall. Beneath my suit we had run a rope and pulley. On top of the building were two guys each holding onto an end of the rope. On my right I was flanked by the two trumpeteers, on my left were 60 students skipping class in order to watch the "rapture."

When everyone was set I gave the signal to the trumpet players. They pointed their horns toward the open window and began playing "When the Roll Is Called up Yonder I'll Be There." But there was a problem. When I gave the signal to the trumpet players, one of the guys on the roof mistook that for his cue, so I began to be raptured sideways! After I had gone about six feet in the air, the other rope guy surmised that he must have missed his cue. So he began pulling his rope at the same time that the first guy, realizing his mistake, let out all his slack. (The rapture nearly became the rupture!)

They quickly got me evened out and as I drifted past the window, I saw 40 students with eyes as big as saucers. With both hands pointed heavenward I yelled, "I'm coming home Jesus, I don't know why they're not, but I'm coming home!"

As the guys dragged me the remaining feet up onto the roof, the crowd cheered. (Students who skip class will clap for just about anything.) On the roof, all three of us were exhausted. I felt as if the brick wall had become a giant emory board and I was a fingernail. The two rope guys were drained from pulling dead weight up two stories.

After a good laugh, they caught their breath. Jim Stanley laughed and said, "Hey, Stone, did you ever think what would have happened if while we were pulling you up, we got raptured and you didn't?"

With a straight face, I replied, "Yes, I did, and that's why I felt safe in choosing you guys!" (I'm not sure that anyone at CBC could remember any sermon that I ever preached but for some reason, they all remember the 'rapture'.)

Regardless of predictions and calculations Jesus reminded us of the truth when he said, "No one knows the day or the hour" (Matthew 24:36). We need to be skeptical of date setters. Knowing that He is coming is more important than when He is coming. That's why we must be ready at all times and constantly preparing others to be ready.

When we were expecting our third child, the night before Beth's due date, I was praying with the girls. My younger daughter interrupted my prayer and said, "Is this the last day?"

Not a bad question for the Christian to ask of God each morning. "Lord, is this the last day?" It could be. That's why we must be ready and that's why we must have an intensity in sharing our faith.

The Bible compares the sudden return of Christ to the birth pangs of an expectant mother. "While people are saying, 'Peace and safety,' destruction will come on them suddenly, as labor pains on a pregnant woman, and they will not escape" (1 Thessalonians 5:1-4).

God stands waiting and willing to forgive. He has patiently postponed His judgment to give us more chances to come to repentance, and more opportunities for people to see and hear a sermon through our lives. Eventually that tolerance of evil will be replaced by justice, and evil will be punished.

The Second Coming will be one of two things for you — either a glorious, joyful, long-awaited victory and reward or an agonizing, terror-filled realization of the truth without provision for another chance. Our relationship to the Lord determines how we will react on that day.

Recently a television reporter asked me a strange question. She said, "How can you tell a Christian from someone who isn't?"

And I got the impression that she meant in a physical sense. So I said, "Well, you can't tell from the outside. Besides, we all put up a false veneer to some extent."

But then I said, "Christians have a peace that passes understanding, because they have placed their hope in the eternal, not the temporary."

But you know what else I could have said? I could have said, "I believe that there will be a time when it will be very obvious who truly is a Christian. That is when Christ returns, for in that split second it will become quite evident those who are encouraged by the sight of their Savior and Lord and those who are terrified at the mistake they have made."

Are you looking to the day of Christ's return with fear or with hope? The New Testament talks about the Second Coming some 300 times. Jesus kept every other promise. Let me assure you He looks forward to keeping this one. Jesus personally guarantees, "And if I go and prepare a place for you, I will come back and take you to be with me that you also may be where I am" (John 14:2-3).

The Bottom Line

Several years ago Billy Graham was Johnny Carson's guest on the "Tonight Show." At one point Carson asked him, "Billy, what do you think would happen if Jesus came to earth again? I'd bet we'd do Him in again."

Billy Graham leaned forward in his seat and said, "You know, Johnny, Jesus predicted that He would return to earth. But the first time He came in love, the next time He'll come in power — no one will do Him in."

Believe me on this, when Jesus returns, he won't have to announce His arrival. He won't have to say anything. When you see a glorified being riding on a cloud with trumpets playing in stereo — trust me, it's Jesus.

What's the world coming to? The world is coming to the day when every knee shall bow and every tongue confess that Jesus Christ is Lord (Philippians 2:10-11).

Over the dome of the Capitol Building in Washington, DC, is the following inscription: "One God, one law, one element, and one far-off divine event toward which the whole creation moves." Be prepared, Jesus is coming again.

Each day you are moving closer to that event. That is why it is imperative that we share with everyone the good news that salvation is available through Jesus Christ. And that is why it is crucial that we match the sermons we preach to the one we live.

Conclusion

What Will People See in You?

Over a year ago I invited one of our local sportscasters and his wife to come to our church's Easter pageant. They came and thoroughly enjoyed it. One of the most powerful parts was a dramatic scene of Jesus healing people. It was an incredibly moving point in the program. When the song concluded as we clapped and wiped our eyes, Fred leaned over and said, "You can't preach that, you have to *see* it." At the time, neither of us had any idea that he was verbalizing the title of this book, *I'd Rather **See** a Sermon.*

Some things aren't as effective when spoken, but when seen they can become very potent, not just in a pageant but more importantly in your daily life. Not everyone listens, but mark it down, everyone watches. The best preachers are the ones whose lives reinforce their sermons.

Maybe that's what prompted preacher Paul to tell preacher Timothy, "Watch your life and doctrine closely. Persevere in them, because if you do, you will save both yourself and your hearers" (1 Timothy 4:16).

In His last words just prior to His ascension, Christ gave a mandate to His followers to share the gospel. They were instructed to baptize those who believe and to con-

147

tinue to help them to grow in the faith. Christ's last concern must be our first priority.

The influence of your life can have an incredible impact. What will people see in you? The Christian has the greatest news in the world to share, but the world isn't going to beat a path to your door to hear it. You, as a Christian, must be open to telling others.

You must play to your strengths and use the skills that God has blessed you with. Your methodology may differ from the way some of your Christian friends try to reach the lost. But remember, there is not a right or wrong way, provided the message of Christ comes through in a loving manner.

You must have a passion for the lost; a desire to share the message of salvation with others. The promise of forgiveness, and the reality of heaven and hell, have a way of motivating you to let unbelievers know what's available through a relationship with Jesus Christ.

Hopefully as you have read through this book several things have happened:

➤ Names and faces of unsaved friends, co-workers, neighbors, and acquaintances have occasionally popped into your mind

➤ Courage has grown within you as you've realized you *can* share your faith

➤ Relief has come over you as you know that your responsibility is to plant seeds and not to personally save people

➤ Prayer has begun, as you ask God to soften the soil of the hearts of those you hope to influence

➤ Excitement has grown as you have discovered many new approaches in sharing Christ that you had not previously considered.

In the past, maybe you have never had the courage or compassion to share your faith with others. You tense up, or wimp out. That was then, this is now. In 1954 on the opening day of major league baseball, the Cincinnati Reds played the Milwaukee Braves. Both teams started one rookie. The rookie for the Reds was Jim Greengrass. On his first day he went 4-4, with four doubles! The Milwaukee rookie was hitless in four trips to the plate. Now that was just the first day, but whose name do you remember? Jim Greengrass, or Hank Aaron? (Greengrass went on to start his own lawn care company.)

My point is that people won't remember how you started, but they will remember how you finished. Paul said, "Forgetting what is behind and straining toward what is ahead" (Philippians 3:13). Regardless of blown opportunities, or missed chances in the past, you can still make a significant and eternal impact on others by beginning to share your faith — from now on.

This just may be the next step in deepening your commitment to Christ. To take your faith which in the past has been private and go public. Now that is risky business because it may change the way people view you.

In John 12 we read the story of Mary pouring a pint of pure nard, a precious perfume, all over the feet of Jesus. The perfume was worth a year's wages. The Gospel accounts tell us that Judas along with the other disciples felt that the perfume should have been sold and the money given to the poor. As they saw Christ's wet feet their attitude seemed to say, "How ridiculous. What a waste!" But what on the surface appeared to be a waste upon closer investigation was true love. Jesus had raised Mary's brother Lazarus from the dead. And instead of trying to put her love into words, she put her love into action. She abandoned talking about love and chose to demonstrate love.

When you decide to introduce others to Jesus you are putting love into action. Your lifestyle becomes the sermon that they will see. Actions speak louder than words. I agree with Edgar A. Guest.

"I'd rather see a sermon than hear one any day,
    I'd rather one should walk with me
        than merely show the way."

How exciting to think that you hold the key to unlocking someone's future. If you will lovingly share Jesus you can impact their lives and their family for generations to come. The best doctor may be able to prolong a person's life for an additional ten, twenty, or maybe thirty years.

But just think, by courageously expressing the difference Christ has made in your life you may help to prolong a life for eternity. To me, that's pretty big news! And it's more than that. For it's not just eternal life in the future, it is also the abundant life in the present.

The Bottom Line of this Book

In Columbia, Missouri, one of the Christian churches has an elder named Paul Rowoth. Years ago on a Saturday, Paul went into a J.C. Penney's store and made a purchase. The clerk gave him his change and said, "Here's some change for Sunday School."

Paul replied, "Yes. By the way do you go to church and Sunday School anywhere?"

She said, "No our family recently moved here and my husband and I haven't started attending anywhere."

So Paul invited them to the Westside Church, and the next day she came. The interesting thing was that my dad, who was the preacher of the church, had called on her several weeks before, at the request of her previous minister who wanted her to try out Westside. But when dad asked her she didn't come. She probably felt that he was simply doing his job and was supposed to be inviting people. But when this man invited her, obviously for no reason except out of concern for her family, that was when she decided to come. Do you know why? Because people would rather see a sermon than hear one, any day. Francis of Assisi said, "Preach the gospel all the time; if necessary, use words."*

---

*Cited by Charles Colson in *The Body* (Dallas: Word, 1992), p. 88.

Suggested Reading

Aldrich, Joseph C. *Gentle Persuasion: Creative Ways to Introduce Your Friends to Christ*. Portland: Multnomah, 1988.

_____. *Life-style Evangelism: Crossing Traditional Boundaries to Reach the Unbelieving World*. Portland: Multnomah, 1981.

Appleby, Jerry L. *Missions Have Come Home to America*. Kansas City: Beacon Hill, 1986.

Arn, Win and Charles Arn. *The Master's Plan for Making Disciples: How Every Christian Can Be an Effective Witness Through an Enabling Church*. Pasadena, CA: Church Growth Press, 1982.

Bayly, Joseph. *The Gospel Blimp*. Grand Rapids: Zondervan, 1960.

Bleecker, Walter S. *The Non-confronter's Guide to Leading a Person to Christ*. San Bernardino: Here's Life, 1990.

Bodey, Richard Allen, Editor. *If I Had Only One Sermon to Preach*. Grand Rapids: Baker, 1994.

Boursier, Helen T. *Tell It with Style: Evangelism for Every Personality Type*. Downers Grove: InterVarsity, 1994.

Briner, Bob. *Roaring Lambs*. Grand Rapids: Zondervan, 1993.

Chaney, Charles. *The Principles and Practice of Indigenous Church Planting*. Nashville: Broadman, 1981.

Clark, Wade, et al. *A Generation of Seekers*. San Francisco: Harper, 1993.

Coleman, Robert E. *The Master Plan of Evangelism*. Old Tappan, NJ: Revell, 1964.

Crawford, Dan R. *EvangeLife: A Guide to Life-style Evangelism*. Nashville: Broadman, 1984.

Eisenman, Tom. *Everyday Evangelism: Making the Most of Life's Common Moments*. Downers Grove: InterVarsity, 1987.

Elias, LeRoy. *One-to-One Evangelism*. Wheaton: Victor, 1990.

Green, Michael. *Evangelism in the Early Church*. Grand Rapids: Eerdmans, 1970.

_____. *One to One: How to Share Your Faith with a Friend*. Nashville: Moorings, 1995.

Hale, J. Russell. *The Unchurched — Who They Are and Why They Stay Away*. San Francisco: Harper & Row, 1980.

Hunter, Kent. *Your Church Has Personality*. Nashville: Abingdon Press, 1988.

Hybels, Bill and Mark Mittelberg. *Becoming a Contagious Christian*. Grand Rapids: Zondervan, 1994.

Keefauver, Larry. *Friends & Faith: Friendship Evangelism in Youth Ministry*. Loveland, CO: Group Books, 1986.

Little, Paul E. *How to Give Away Your Faith*. Downers Grove: InterVarsity, 1966.

Petersen, Jim. *Evangelism Is A Lifestyle*. Colorado Springs: NavPress, 1980.

Pippert, Rebecca Manley. *Out of the Saltshaker and into the World*. Downers Grove: InterVarsity, 1979.

Ridenour, Fritz. *How to Be a Christian Without Being Religious*. Glendale, CA: Regal, 1967.

Schaller, Lyle. *Activating the Passive Church: Diagnosis and Treatment*. Nashville: Abingdon, 1981.

Sjogren, Steve. *Conspiracy of Kindness*. Ann Arbor: Servant, 1993.

About the Author

David Stone is Preaching Associate with Southeast Christian Church in Louisville, Kentucky. His sermons are distributed across the country through the Living Word tape ministry. He has been Youth Minister at Shively Christian Church in Louisville, Kentucky and Director of Admissions at Cincinnati Bible College. Dave has written lessons for *The Christian Standard*, Youth Curriculum for Standard Publishing and contributed to several publications for Cincinnati Bible College and Seminary.

Dave received the B.A. in Christian Ministries from Cincinnati Bible College. He has served as Trustee for CBC&S since 1991 and as a member of the North American Christian Convention Committee since 1995, and the Executive Committee since 1996. In addition to his preaching responsibilities he is the staff representative for Southeast's Relocation Project, including a 9,100 seat sanctuary.

He and his wife, Beth, have three children, Savannah, Sadie, and Samuel. Dave enjoys golf and doing motivational speaking and comedy for businesses and secular audiences.